atoes & Yams Finishin...
...s The Paul Mayer Method Artic...
...lery Root Green Peppers Brocc...
...els Sprouts Cauliflower Aspara...
...Onions Cucumbers Eggplant B...
...pinach Finishing Touches Carro...
...es Cabbage Squash Leeks Sw...
...rtichokes Asparagus Mushroo...
...gplant Brussels Sprouts Caulifl...
...r Cabbage Unusual Vegetables ...
...ery Broccoli Green Beans Squa...
...ushrooms Onions Leeks Potat...

nitty gritty books

Chicken Cookbook	Soups & Stews	To My Daughter With Love
Skillet Cookbook	Crepes & Omelets	Natural Foods
Convection Oven	Microwave Cooking	Chinese Vegetarian
Household Hints	Vegetable Cookbook	The Jewish Cookbook
Seafood Cookbook	Kid's Arts and Crafts	Working Couples
Quick Breads	Bread Baking	Mexican
Pasta & Rice	The Crockery Pot Cookbook	Sunday Breakfast
Calorie Watchers Cookbook	Classic Greek Cooking	Fisherman's Wharf Cookbook
Pies & Cakes	Low Carbohydrate Cookbook	Barbecue Cookbook
Yogurt	Kid's Cookbook	Ice Cream Cookbook
The Ground Beef Cookbook	Italian	Blender Cookbook
Cocktails & Hors d'Oeuvres	Cheese Guide & Cookbook	The Wok, a Chinese Cookbook
Casseroles & Salads	Miller's German	Japanese Country
Pressure Cooking	Quiche & Souffle	Fondue Cookbook
Food Processor Cookbook		

designed with giving in mind

It has been said that meat-eating begets ferocious dispositions while vegetables accentuate the gentler affections.

Vegetable

cookbook

by PAUL MAYER

Illustrated by CRAIG TORLUCCI

A Nitty Gritty Book*
Published by
Nitty Gritty Productions
P.O. Box 5457
Concord, California

*Nitty Gritty Books - Trademark
Owned by Nitty Gritty Productions
Concord, California

ISBN 0-911954-34-1

Contents

Introduction

One of the most beautiful sights in any market are the rows of bright, fresh vegetables. Yellow squash, gleaming purple eggplants, green petaled artichokes and oyster white mushrooms combine with the many other colors and textures to provide a beautiful vision for the shopper to enjoy.

Artists paint vegetables and we paper our walls with patterns of them, yet in spite of their beauty and their well known nutritional value, vegetables are not the favorite food of most children and a surprisingly large number of adults. Why?

Any poorly prepared food is not pleasurable to eat, and this is particularly true of vegetables. Because they require more attention and ingenuity from the chef to bring out their full flavor and retain their texture, they are too often poorly prepared. Vegetables are delicious and extremely attractive when the proper attention is given to them. A method we recommend for cooking green vegetables is the Paul Mayer Method which is given in detail on page 4. Cooked this way, vegetables retain their beautiful green color and delicious, flavor.

The recipes presented in this book were selected from the files of the Paul Mayer Cooking School in San Francisco, California, with the exception of those provided by Nitty Gritty and identified by an asterisk (*) next to each one in the Index.

While their names and preparation may differ, many of the same vegetables are found throughout the world. Their interesting origin is discussed briefly in the introducion of each chapter.

2

Nowhere else in the world will one find the profusion of fresh produce that is available in the United States. When the season is over in the northern states, the same crop is just ready for harvesting in a warmer, southern climate. Rapid transportation moves vegetables from warm climates to cold ones and almost every vegetable is available the year around. Some vegetables are even shipped in from Mexico when out of season here. Asparagus remains seasonal and artichokes still grow primarily in one area, but modern technology and transportation have made great strides in expanding the availability of produce. In fact, there are so many vegetables, it is impossible to cover them all in this collection.

The vegetables and recipes selected are those most popular throughout the country, and commonly found in backyard gardens. For variety, a few of the more uncommon ones have been included.

Fresh vegetables are featured, but frozen ones can be substituted in most cases. Here is a unique collection of recipes. Some are simple, some are more complex, some are entrees, some go well with sauced dishes and some go best with simple entrees. All will intrigue you and help to prove that vegetables can taste delicious as well as look beautiful.

3

The Paul Mayer Method

FOR COOKING GREEN VEGETABLES

This 7 minute method for cooking fresh peas, green beans, asparagus, broccoli and Brussels sprouts produces attractive, delicious vegetables which retain their bright green color. The secret is to have the water boiling when the vegetables are added and to keep it boiling during the entire cooking process as follows:

4

1. Bring a teakettle full of water to a full boil.

2. Into another pot with a lid, scatter a handful of sugar and 1 teaspoon of salt. Place over high heat until sugar begins to caramelize.

3. Quickly add prepared vegetables. Without reducing heat, pour in the boiling water. The water never ceases boiling and the vegetables start cooking immediately. Cover the pot and boil rapidly for exactly 7 minutes.

4. Quickly drain vegetables into a colander and rinse briefly with cool tap water to stop the cooking action. The vegetables will remain hot!

5. Drain well and season with melted butter, or serve with the Almond Crumb Topping on page 13, or one of the sauces or seasoned butters given in the Finishing Touches section which follows.
This method is not used for root vegetables, eggplant, artichokes or spinach.

5

Finishing Touches

DILL SAUCE FOR VEGETABLES

1/4 cup olive oil   2 tbs. fresh dill <u>or</u>

1 tbs. lemon juice   1 tsp. dried dill weed

    Blend ingredients with wire whip until creamy. Pour over cooked, hot vegetables. Makes 4 servings.

6

GREEK SAUCE FOR VEGETABLES

1/4 cup fresh lemon juice   1/4 cup olive oil   1/2 tsp. salt

    Combine lemon juice, oil and salt. Whisk or shake in a container until smooth and creamy. Drizzle sauce over hot, well-drained vegetables. Makes enough for 4 servings. Excellent with cauliflower, Brussels sprouts, artichokes, broccoli and spinach.

BLENDER MAYONNAISE

3 whole eggs
2-1/4 tsp. salt
1-1/2 tsp. dry mustard
pinch paprika

6 tbs. white vinegar or
6 tbs. lemon juice or
3 tbs. of each
3-1/2 cups oil

Place eggs, salt, mustard, paprika, vinegar (or lemon juice, or a combination) and 3/4 cup oil in blender container. Cover. Blend on highest speed 5 seconds or until mixed. Remove cap from cover. Start adding oil in a slow but steady stream. Pour directly into the center of the whirlpool formed by the swirling mixture. Pour steadily until the whirlpool disappears completely. This should use 1-1/2 to 2 cups of the oil. Continue adding oil, a little at a time. The mayonnaise will become thicker and thicker. Add the oil in this manner until it is all gone. Never add more oil until each addition is completely worked in. Keep blender on highest speed all the time. Makes 1 quart.

HOLLANDAISE SAUCE

2 egg yolks	salt, cayenne papper to taste
1-2 tbs. lemon juice	1/2 cup (1/4 lb.) butter, melted

Place egg yolks, lemon juice, salt and cayenne in blender container. Cover. Blend on low speed 5 seconds. Remove cap. Pour in butter in a slow, steady stream. Continue blending only until sauce has thickened. (Should it curdle, add 2 additional egg yolks. Blend at high speed while adding whipping cream 1 tablespoon at a time until sauce reconstitutes.) Makes about 1 cup.

CHANTILLY SAUCE

1/2 cup whipping cream
1 cup Hollandaise Sauce

Whip cream until stiff. Gently fold into Hollandaise. Makes 2 cups.

SOUFFLED HOLLANDAISE

1 cup Hollandaise Sauce   2 egg whites

Prepare sauce. Just before serving time, beat egg whites until stiff, but not dry. Fold into Hollandaise. Spoon over any cooked vegetable of your choice. (Asparagus and broccoli are especially delicious with this sauce.) Place under hot broiler 3 to 4 minutes or until golden. Serve immediately. Makes about 2 cups.

9

MOCK HOLLANDAISE

1/2 cup mayonnaise   1/4 tsp. salt
3 tbs. cream   1 tbs. lemon juice

Mix mayonnaise, cream and salt in a measuring cup. Set cup in a saucepan. Add 2 or 3 inches of hot water to pan. Heat sauce about 5 minutes. Add lemon juice. Stir and serve. Makes about 2/3 cup.

MORNAY SAUCE

1/4 cup butter
1/4 cup flour
1-3/4 cups half & half
salt, cayenne pepper to taste
1 cup grated Parmesan cheese
2 egg yolks, beaten

10   Melt butter in saucepan. Remove from heat and add flour. Blend in cream and seasonings. Cook over medium heat until mixture boils. Add cheese and continue cooking until melted. If sauce is too thick, thin with a little milk. Add a little of the hot sauce to egg yolks. Quickly stir back into sauce. Remove from heat and use as directed. Makes 6 servings.

TANGY CHEESE SAUCE

2 tbs. butter
2 tbs. flour
1/2 tsp. salt
pinch pepper, paprika
1 cup light cream or milk
1 cup (4 oz.) grated sharp cheddar
1 tbs. Dijon-style mustard

11

Measure butter, flour, seasonings and cream into blender container. Cover and blend on high speed 15 to 30 seconds. Add cheese and blend 15 seconds longer. Pour into saucepan. Cook over medium heat until mixture boils. Stir in mustard and serve over cooked, hot vegetables. Makes 6 servings.

LEMON BUTTER

1/4 cup butter   dash cayenne
1 tbs. fresh lemon juice   1 tbs. finely chopped parsley
1/2 tsp. salt

    Melt butter. Add remaining ingredients. Heat and serve over cooked, hot vegetables. Makes 4 servings.

12

HERB BUTTER

1/2 cup butter   1/4 tsp. salt
1 clove garlic, minced   freshly ground pepper
1/4 tsp. oregano   1/4 cup fresh lemon juice

    Melt butter in small saucepan. Add garlic and seasonings. Stir in lemon juice. Heat and pour over hot cooked vegetables. Makes 6 servings.

ONION BUTTER

2 tbs. dehydrated onion soup mix   1 tbs. minced chives or parsley
1 cup (1/2 lb.) butter or margarine

Blend ingredients thoroughly. Put into covered container. Keep in refrigerator and use as needed. Makes 1-1/4 cups.

ALMOND CRUMB TOPPING

1/4 cup butter   1 cup soft bread crumbs
1 clove garlic, minced   seasoned salt to taste
1/2 cup almonds

Melt butter in skillet. Add garlic, almonds and crumbs. Saute until almonds are golden and crumbs are crisp. Add salt, if desired. Serve over cooked vegetables. Makes 6 servings.

Artichokes

Artichokes originated in the Mediterranean area and were first cultivated in Sicily and Italy. Ancient Romans were known to have preserved the small ones in brine, much as we do today. Centuries later, Catherine De Medici is credited with introducing artichokes to France when she became the bride of the future king, Henry II. In turn, French colonists brought artichokes to America. Eventually the coastal area of Northern California, where the buds are, "kissed by the fog," became known as the Artichoke Capital of the World. Artichokes are a member of the thistle family and are actually a bud which, when allowed to stay on the plant, opens up into a beautiful purple thistle. Artichokes are available almost all year, but the peak season is between March and May. They are low in calories and provide small quantities of various vitamins and minerals.

SELECTING — Look for compact artichokes with tightly closed leaves and a fresh, bright green color. They should feel crisp, not limp. If the artichoke has started to spread open, it is overmature and on the verge of wilting due to loss of moisture. It will rapidly shrivel and turn brown. In the winter, sometimes even the freshest artichokes may have brown spots on the outside leaves due to changes in the weather, especially if the temperature suddenly drops below freezing. This does not affect the inside leaves. Artichokes are usually sold singly or as a unit. Sometimes you will see them by the pound, especially the very small ones which come from the bottom of the stem and are often referred to as artichoke hearts. These are also the ones which are canned and frozen. Allow 1 medium or large artichoke per serving. Huge ones are sometimes cut lengthwise to make 2 servings.

STORING — Do not wash artichokes until ready to cook them. Keep in the refrigerator tightly wrapped in plastic or sealed in a plastic bag. Fresh artichokes which are in prime condition will keep up to 2 weeks.

PREPARING AND COOKING — Rinse artichokes and soak in warm water 10 to 15 minutes to remove any foreign matter. Trim stem even with the bottom so they will sit flat. Remove small bottom leaves. Cut thorny point off even with the tops of the first leaves. Then cut off about a third of each leaf to remove their thorns and make them look attractive. Scissors are best to use for this procedure. If desired, the choke can be removed at this time by gently spreading the leaves and pulling out the light-colored, center leaves. Then scrape out the fuzzy part with a spoon. Since artichokes have a tendency to discolor when cut, rub the cut parts with lemon or prepare a mixture of 3 tablespoons vinegar to each quart of water. Submerge the trimmed artichokes in this acid solution until all are ready to be cooked. The same water can be seasoned more and used for cooking the artichokes. There are different methods for cooking artichokes, but two of the most popular are steam-boiling and boiling in a quantity of water.

To steam-boil, put an inch or two of fresh water in a large kettle. Add 1 to 2 tablespoons lemon juice or vinegar, 1 clove garlic, 1 teaspoon salt, 5 to 6 peppercorns and 1 to 2 tablespoons olive or salad oil. Cover and bring to boil. Stand artichokes up in water. Cover pan and steam-boil about 25 to 35 minutes for medium-sized ones, and 40 to 50 minutes for large ones. They are done when bottoms can be easily pierced with a fork and leaves pull out easily. Take care not to overcook artichokes as the edible parts will become mushy. When done, remove from pot and turn upside down to drain. Serve hot or cold.

To boil, bring a large kettle of fresh water, with seasonings and oil added, to boil. Drop in artichokes and place a plate on top to keep them under the water while cooking. Cooking times will be approximately the same as for the steam-boiling method. Lift from water and turn upside down to drain. Use as desired.

18 **SERVING AND EATING** — Serve artichokes upright on a plate with sauce for dipping. If the choke has been removed, the sauce may be served right in the hollow. Special artichoke plates are available which hold the artichoke in the center and provide a space for sauce and the discarded leaves. While not a necessity, they are very nice to have.

Artichokes are eaten with the fingers! Pull off the leaves, one at a time, and dip into a sauce. Only the light green part at the base of each leaf is eaten. This is done by drawing the bottom of the leaf between your teeth. The rest of leaf is discarded. This process is continued until all leaves are gone and only the center part remains. If the choke or fuzzy part has not been removed, it should be scooped out with a spoon and discarded. The delicious part which is left is known as the artichoke bottom and, unlike the rest of the artichoke, it is eaten with a fork. Cut into bite-sized pieces and dip in sauce.

Artichoke bottoms are used in many ways. Several receipes using these delicious morsels are given on the following pages. They can be purchased in jars or cans, or be prepared from fresh artichokes. To do this, buy the largest artichokes you can find and cook them until tender. Then pull away the leaves and remove the chokes. The remaining bottoms should then be trimmed until smooth and attractive. They have a natural "hollow" for holding a filling. (Sometime try substituting artichoke bottoms for the English muffins usually used in Eggs Benedict!) The trimmed away leaves can be chilled and arranged petal-fashion around a sauce, used as garnish or in Artichoke Petal Salad on page 30. Never throw away any edible parts of an artichoke. They can be used in many delicious ways, even for making soup.

ARTICHOKES A LA GRECQUES

This dish, with its hearty filling is a meal in itself. Served with crispy bread and a tangy salad, it will satisfy even the most demanding appetites. No sauce is needed, but if desired, the basting stock may be strained and used for dipping the artichoke leaves.

6 large artichokes
lemon
salt
6 whole peppercorns
1 bay leaf
3 tbs. tarragon vinegar
8 tbs. butter
18 chicken livers
3 medium onions, finely chopped
1-1/2 cups finely chopped tongue
1-1/2 cups finely chopped mushrooms

3 tbs. chopped parsley
freshly ground pepper
2 tbs. tomato paste
1-1/2 tsp. Bovril
3 tbs. flour
1 cup stock
6 slices bacon
bread crumbs
6 tsp. grated Parmesan cheese
6 firm mushrooms

Trim artichokes and rub the cuts with lemon. Cook in plenty of boiling water with salt, peppercorns, bay leaf and vinegar 30 minutes to 1 hour, depending on size. Artichokes are done when inside leaves pull away easily. Remove from water. Invert to drain. Spread artichokes open and remove the light-colored, cone-shaped center leaves, and scrape out chokes with a spoon. Melt 4 tablespoons butter in a large skillet. When it is smoking, brown livers quickly. Remove and add onions and chopped mushrooms. Cook slowly about 5 minutes, then add tongue. Chop livers and return to pan. Add parsley, salt, pepper, tomato paste and Bovril. Blend in flour. Add 6 tablespoons stock and cook a few moments. Fill artichokes with mixture. Wrap each with bacon. Set in baking pan and pour in remaining stock. Cook 20 to 25 minutes in 375°F oven. Baste frequently. Remove and sprinkle tops with bread crumbs and grated cheese. Dot each with 1 teaspoon butter. Brown under a heated broiler. While artichokes are baking, saute mushroom caps in the remaining two tablespoons butter. Place a mushroom cap on each artichoke for garnish. Makes 6 servings.

ARTICHOKE BOTTOMS WITH GREEN BEANS

A splendid accompaniment for your favorite roast.

1 large jar (15 oz.) artichoke bottoms*
1 lb. green beans
5 tbs. butter
1/4 cup flour
3/4 cup whipping cream
salt and cayenne pepper
1 tsp. lemon juice
2 egg yolks
6 tbs. grated Gruyere cheese

Drain artichoke bottoms and reserve 1/2 cup liquid. Run beans through a French slicer. Cut slices into 2-1/2 inch lengths. Cook according to the Paul Mayer Method on page 4. Drain beans. Reserve 1/2 cup cooking liquid. Melt 2 tablespoons butter in a heavy saucepan. Remove pan from heat. Blend in flour.

Stir in artichoke liquor, bean liquor and 1/2 cup cream. Season highly with salt and cayenne pepper. Return to heat. Stir until it boils. Add lemon juice. Beat egg yolks into remaining cream and add a little hot sauce. Then stir mixture rapidly back into sauce. Stir in green beans. Saute artichoke bottoms in 3 tablespoons foaming butter. Place in flameproof serving dish. Spoon green bean mixture onto bottoms. Sprinkle with Gruyere. Run dish under heated broiler until cheese is melted, crusted and browned. Makes 6 servings.

23

*If using fresh artichokes, prepare 6 very large ones as directed on page 19.

ARTICHOKES MARIE LOUISE

An unusual combination to be enjoyed even by those who aren't fond of rice.

1/2 cup long grain rice
1/4 lb. butter
2 cups coarsely chopped onion
1 cup chicken stock
1 cup finely chopped mushrooms
1/2 cup whipping cream
salt and pepper
juice of 1 lemon
1-1/2 tsp. flour
2 truffles, finely minced
8 cooked artichoke bottoms

24

Cook rice in 4 cups boiling water for 5 minutes. Drain and set aside. In a deep Dutch oven, melt 4 tablespoons of butter. Add onions and cook slowly over low heat until soft but not brown. Stir in rice. Add chicken stock and bring to boil. Cover Dutch oven and place in 325°F oven 1 hour. Then force the mixture through a food mill and set aside. Melt 2 tablespoons butter in a skillet. Add mushrooms and cook until tender. Add whipping cream. Season to taste with salt, pepper and lemon juice. Knead together 1-1/2 teaspoons butter and flour. Add this beurre manie to the boiling liquid. Cook, stirring constantly, until mixture thickens. Mix mushrooms with rice and adjust seasoning. Add half of chopped truffles. Sprinkle artichoke bottoms with salt and pepper. Brush with remaining butter, melted. Place filling in a pastry bag fitted with a star tube. Squeeze filling onto artichoke bottoms. Sprinkle with remaining chopped truffle. Place in a buttered, shallow ovenproof serving dish. Bake in 375°F oven 25 minutes. Makes 8 servings.

ARTICHOKE BOTTOMS WITH MUSHROOMS

6 large artichoke bottoms	1/4 cup flour
1 lb. mushrooms	salt, pepper, basil
12 tbs. butter	1 tbs. tomato paste
1 onion, finely chopped	1/2 cup beef stock
1 green pepper, finely chopped	6 tsp. freshly grated Parmesan

26   Cook artichoke bottoms and pat dry. Chop mushrooms finely. Squeeze firmly in a towel to extract all juice. Melt 1/2 cup butter in large skillet. When very hot, saute chopped mushrooms over high heat until nicely browned. Add onion and green pepper and continue cooking slowly until vegetables are soft. Remove pan from heat and add flour. Season with salt, black pepper and basil. Add tomato paste. Gradually stir in stock. Return to heat and stir constantly until mixture thickens and boils. Saute artichoke bottoms in remaining butter until nicely browned on both sides. Fill with mushroom mixture and arrange on a flameproof serving dish. Sprinkle tops with cheese. Run dish under heated broiler until nicely browned. Makes 6 servings.

ARTICHOKE BOTTOMS STUFFED WITH PUREED PEAS

6 pkg. (10 oz. ea.) frozen peas
12 tbs. butter
9 tbs. flour
2 cups (1 pt.) whipping cream
salt and white pepper

Tabasco sauce
sugar
6 huge artichoke bottoms
1 cup grated Parmesan cheese
cayenne pepper

Cook peas according to package directions. Drain well. Force through a food mill or strainer. Stir in 1/2 cup butter, flour and 1 cup cream. Place mixture in blender container. Cover and puree. Season with salt, pepper, Tabasco and a little sugar. Place puree in saucepan. Stir over medium heat until mixture boils. Lower heat and cook 3 minutes, stirring constantly. Melt remaining butter in heavy skillet. When it is foaming, saute artichoke bottoms on both sides. Drain well. Fill with puree, mounding it high on each bottom. Whip remaining cream and mix with cheese. Season with salt and cayenne. Spoon on top of filled artichokes. Run under heated broiler until cream is melted and browned. Serve at once. Makes 6 servings.

ARTICHOKE BOTTOMS STUFFED WITH SPINACH

This two-in-one vegetable, which puts together two of my favorite dishes, goes especially well with roast beef, steak, baked salmon and fillet of sole.

Spinach Barnet, page 155
6 huge artichokes
1 lemon
salt
6 peppercorns
3 tbs. tarragon vinegar
1 bay leaf
1/4 cup butter
6 tbs. grated Parmesan cheese

28

Prepare Spinach Barnet as directed, omitting the hard cooked eggs. Trim tips from artichoke leaves. Cut off stems and score bottoms. Rub all cuts with lemon to prevent them from darkening. Cook artichokes in boiling, salted water with peppercorns, vinegar and bay leaf added, until leaves pull out easily and bottom is tender when pierced with a fork. Remove artichokes from water. Invert until well drained. Pull off leaves and save for another use. Scrape out fuzzy chokes with a teaspoon. Trim bottoms. Melt butter in large skillet. When it is foaming, saute artichoke bottoms until nicely browned. Fill with Spinach Barnet. Sprinkle with cheese and run under a heated broiler to brown. Serve immediately. Makes 6 servings.

ARTICHOKE PETAL SALAD

This salad is an excellent way to use artichoke leaves left over when preparing fresh artichoke bottoms for another purpose.

1-1/3 cups oil
2/3 cup vinegar
1 tsp. salt
1/4 tsp. pepper
1/4 tsp. oregano
1/8 tsp. paprika
1 bay leaf, crumbled
1 clove garlic
1/2 lb. cooked shrimp
leaves from 6 cooked artichokes*
6 thick tomato slices
2 avocados, sliced

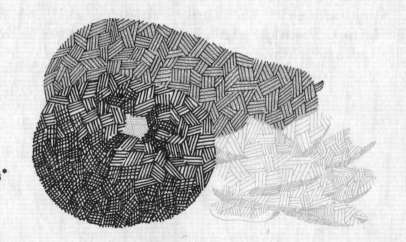

In large mixing bowl combine oil and vinegar. Add salt, pepper, oregano, paprika, bay leaf and garlic through a press. Beat until blended. Measure off 1/2 cup and combine with shrimp in small bowl. Stir well so that each shrimp is coated. Cover and refrigerate. Put artichoke leaves into large bowl of marinade. Stir to coat each leaf well. Cover and refrigerate several hours or overnight. Stir both mixtures occasionally. When ready to serve, lift shrimp and leaves from marinade. Arrange artichoke leaves petal fashion in a circle on individual salad plates. Place tomato slices in the center of petals. Lay avocado slices on top of tomatoes and top with marinated shrimp. Spoon a little of the marinade over salads. Serve very cold. Pass extra marinade in small bowl or pitcher. Makes 6 servings.

*If artichokes are cooked especially for this salad, trim and marinate the artichoke bottoms along with the leaves. Use in place of the avocados.

Asparagus

Asparagus originated in the eastern Mediterranean and is believed to have been taken to England, among other places, by the ancient Romans. Eventually it came to America with the early settlers. These delicious green spears which we enjoy so much are actually the edible shoots of asparagus plants, which are members of the lily-of-the-valley family.

Asparagus is probably the most seasonal vegetable we have in the United States. To many of us, asparagus and spring are synonymous. Although it sometimes can be found out-of-season, it is usually not of good quality and extremely expensive. It can also be bought frozen and canned, but to me nothing can compare with the taste and texture of fresh. For some reason, the height of elegance in many European restaurants, especially German ones, is a garnish of canned white asparagus. White asparagus, by the way, is created by keeping the spears covered with earth as they develop so they are never exposed to sunlight. They must be peeled from stem to stern before cooking and then they are delicate and delicious. Without this essential, preliminary preparation, they are tough, bitter and disappointing.

SELECTING — Look for firm, straight stalks with well-formed, tightly-closed tips. The stalks should be green about two-thirds of their length, with some white on the stem end. This tough white portion is left on to help the stalks retain their moisture and stay crisp. Avoid limp, wilted spears. As the season progresses, stalks of all sizes will appear on the market. Large thick ones are certainly more impressive looking, but the thinner ones have less waste and are often sweeter and more tender. Asparagus is priced by the pound or bunch. Allow about 1/2 pound of untrimmed asparagus per serving.

STORING — Do not wash asparagus until ready to cook it. Wrap stem ends in damp paper towels and slip into a plastic bag to hold the moisture in. Store in the refrigerator. Use as soon as possible.

PREPARING AND COOKING — Snap off the tough stem-ends of asparagus by holding a spear in both hands and bending. It will break easily where the tender and tough parts meet. What is left of the tip end can be eaten in its entirety. Cook asparagus according to the Paul Mayer Method on page 4.

ASPARAGUS WITH ITALIAN-STYLE TOMATO SAUCE

Baked asparagus is unusual, to say the least. This delicious dish can be prepared ahead and baked when needed. It goes especially well with veal dishes.

1-1/2 lbs. asparagus
3 tbs. melted butter
2 tbs. onion, finely chopped
2 tbs. celery, finely chopped
1 tbs. grated Parmesan cheese

1 tbs. soft bread crumbs
1 can (8 oz.) Italian-style tomatoes
salt and black papper
pinch sugar, thyme, oregano

Wash asparagus well. Break off tough ends. Pour melted butter into oven-proof dish. Lay asparagus in even rows in the bottom of the dish. Scatter onion, celery, cheese and bread crumbs over asparagus. Remove tomatoes from their juice. Chop and combine again with the juice. Season with salt, pepper, sugar and herbs. Pour over contents of baking dish. Bake in 375°F oven 35 to 40 minutes or until asparagus is tender. Makes 6 servings.

ASPARAGUS CHANTILLY

If you like asparagus with hollandaise sauce, you will love this "lily-gilded" version made more delicate by the addition of whipped cream.

Sauce Chantilly, page 8
2 lbs. asparagus
3 tbs. grated Parmesan cheese

Prepare Chantilly Sauce according to the recipe. Thoroughly wash asparagus. Snap off tough ends. Cook spears according to the Paul Mayer Method on page 4. Drain and arrange on a flameproof serving dish. Mask asparagus with Chantilly Sauce, leaving tips uncovered. Sprinkle with Parmesan and run dish under heated broiler until browned. Makes 6 servings.

ASPARAGUS VINAIGRETTE

2 lbs. asparagus
2 to 3 tbs. kosher-style dill pickle pieces
1 cup olive oil
1/2 cup tarragon vinegar
salt and pepper to taste
pinch dry mustard, paprika
2 to 3 tbs. <u>each</u> capers and chives

Cook asparagus according to the Paul Mayer Method on page 4. Drain and dry with paper towels. Remove seeds from pickles and chop very fine. Combine with remaining ingredients. Chill. To serve, arrange chilled asparagus on salad plates. Spoon dressing over asparagus spears. Serve well chilled. Makes 6 to 8 servings.

ASPARAGUS TARTS

Pastry, page 39
2 cups (1 pt.) whipping cream
1 bay leaf
4 sprigs parsley
4 thin onion slices
thyme and marjoram

3 tbs. butter
1/4 lb. lean veal, ground
1 lb. cooked asparagus
1/2 cup grated Gruyere cheese
dry bread crumbs

38

Prepare pastry shell as directed on page 39. Combine cream in a heavy saucepan with bay leaf, parsley, onion slices and a pinch of each herb. Do not add salt. Simmer gently 15 minutes. Melt 1 tablespoon butter in another saucepan. Add veal and cook 2 minutes, stirring constantly. Strain seasoned cream. Add it gradually to the veal. Stir until the mixture begins to boil. Lower heat and simmer 30 minutes, stirring occasionally to prevent scorching. Line bottom of the baked pastry shell with a layer of asparagus, points in. Just barely cover asparagus with a layer of sauce. Arrange another layer of tips, points out this time. Blend cheese into remaining sauce. Pour into shell. Sprinkle with bread crumbs. Dot with remaining butter. Bake in hot oven 475°F until crumbs brown and pie is heated through. Makes 6 servings.

PASTRY

1-1/2 cups flour
3 tbs. butter
3 tbs. Crisco

1/8 tsp. salt
3-1/2 tbs. milk (approximately)

Measure flour into bowl. Add butter and Crisco. Work into flour, along with salt, until mixture resembles coarse meal. Start adding milk, one tablespoon at a time until the dough just gathers. Do not clutch at dough, but move it gently until it comes together. Roll it out between 2 sheets of waxed paper. Fit it into a 10-inch pie plate. Flute edges nicely. Prick crust all over with the tines of a fork. Bake in 375°F oven until nicely browned. Remove to rack to cool.

TOAST CUPS WITH ASPARAGUS

Asparagus prepared in this creamy, tomato-herb sauce can stand alone as a luncheon dish, or supply both starch and vegetable to accompany roasts of all descriptions.

10 slices firm white bread	sugar
3/4 cup melted butter	pinch thyme, oregano, sweet basil
2 bunches asparagus	1/4 cup flour
4 tbs. butter	milk
2 tbs. onion, finely chopped	4 egg yolks
2 tbs. celery, finely chopped	1/4 cup cream
1 can (16 oz.) Italian-style tomatoes	1/4 cup grated Parmesan cheese
salt and black pepper	

Remove crusts from 8 slices of bread. Make crumbs of the remaining two slices. Place bread slices between two pieces of waxed paper. Roll with a rolling pin to make as thin as possible. Saturate rolled slices with melted butter. Press them over the backs of muffin tins. Place in 375°F oven 20 to 30 minutes, or until bread is toasted and browned through. Allow to stand 5 minutes before unmolding. Arrange toast cups on a flameproof serving dish. Wash asparagus thoroughly. Remove tough stem ends. Cook by the Paul Mayer Method on page 4. Melt 4 tablespoons butter in a large skillet. Add onion and celery and saute until vegetables are soft but not brown. Drain tomatoes and save juice. Chop tomatoes and add to skillet. Continue cooking until mixture is well reduced. Season highly with salt, pepper and herbs. Remove from heat and add flour. Add enough milk to the reserved tomato liquid to make 1-1/2 cups. Blend into skillet mixture. Return to heat and stir until sauce boils. Beat egg yolks into cream. Add a little of the hot sauce and pour this mixture back into the skillet, stirring rapidly. Cut asparagus into small pieces and add to the sauce. Reheat without boiling. Spoon into toast cups. Combine bread crumbs and cheese. Sprinkle over filled cups and brown under the broiler. Serve at once. Makes 8 servings.

Broccoli

Broccoli has been popular in Italy and Greece for at least 2,000 years but was almost unknown in the United States before 1920. Brought here by Italian immigrants, it is now one of our most popular vegetables. For some unknown reason, it is never served in France. Broccoli is a member of the cabbage family and is high in vitamins C and A with fair amounts of riboflavin, iron, calcium and potassium. It is available all year.

SELECTING — Look for compact clusters of dark green, tightly-closed buds. Yellow buds indicate overmaturity. Stalks should be firm and not too large. Usually sold by the bunch. Allow 1/3 to 1/2 pound per serving.

STORING — Refrigerate, unwashed, in a plastic bag. Will keep 4 to 5 days.

PREPARING AND COOKING — Rinse and trim leaves and stalk ends. Remove tough layer from stalk with vegetable peeler. If stalks are large, cut several slashes almost to bud clusters. Cut large bunches in half or quarters. Cook according to the Paul Mayer Method on page 4.

BROCCOLI A LA SAN FRANCISCO

2 lbs. broccoli
melted butter
Parmesan cheese
3 tbs. butter
3 tbs. flour
salt, cayenne pepper, celery salt
1 cup milk
1 tbs. lemon juice
3 tbs. orange juice
1 tbs. grated orange rind
1 tsp. grated lemon rind
heavy cream
blanched slivered almonds

44

Wash and trim broccoli. Remove tough portions of stems with a vegetable peeler. Cook according to the Paul Mayer Method on page 4. Drain and quick-

ly rinse in cold water to prevent further cooking. Drain thoroughly. Dip cooked broccoli in melted butter. Sprinkle liberally with Parmesan. Arrange on a
flameproof serving dish. Melt 3 tablespoons butter in saucepan. Stir in flour,
salt, cayenne and celery salt. Cook 1 minute. Remove from heat. Blend in
milk. Return to heat and stir until mixture thickens and boils. Add juices,
grated rinds and just enough cream to thin the sauce a bit and give it a
creamy consistency. Spread carefully over broccoli. Bake in hot oven 425°F
until sauce and almonds are both browned and dish is bubbling. Serve immediately. Makes 6 servings.

45

BROCCOLI WITH CHEESE CUSTARD

1 lb. broccoli
3 eggs
2/3 cup milk
1-1/4 cups grated sharp cheddar cheese
salt and pepper to taste

46

Wash and trim broccoli. Cook according to the Paul Mayer Method on page 4. Drain well and place in buttered shallow casserole. Beat eggs. Add milk, cheese, salt and pepper. Blend and pour over broccoli. Set casserole in another pan with about 1 inch of hot water. Bake in moderate 350°F oven 30 minutes, or until custard is set. Makes 4 servings.

BROCCOLI WITH ALMONDS IN WINE SAUCE

1-1/2 lbs. broccoli
1 bouillon cube
3/4 cup boiling water
1/4 cup butter
1/4 cup flour
1 cup cream

2 tbs. sherry
2 tbs. lemon juice
1/2 tsp. Accent
pepper to taste
1/4 cup Parmesan cheese
1/4 cup toasted slivered almonds

Wash and trim broccoli. Cook according to the Paul Mayer Method on page 4. Drain well. Place in shallow baking dish. Dissolve bouillon cube in water. Melt butter in saucepan. Add flour and stir until mixture bubbles. Remove from heat. Slowly blend in bouillon and cream. Return to medium heat. Cook, stirring constantly, until mixture thickens and comes to a boil. Add sherry, lemon juice, Accent and pepper. Pour over broccoli. Sprinkle on cheese and almonds. Bake in 375°F oven 20 minutes or until thoroughly heated. Makes 6 servings.

Brussels Sprouts

Brussels sprouts are a member of the cabbage family whose origin was in northern Europe around Brussels, Belgium. Grown mostly in California, the peak season is January through March. High in vitamins C and A.

SELECTING — Look for small, firm, bright green heads. Avoid large spongy ones with yellow leaves. Usually sold loose and priced by the pound or by the container, if packaged. Allow 1/3 to 1/2 pound per serving.

STORING — Do not wash until ready to cook. Place in a plastic bag and refrigerate. Use within 1 or 2 days.

PREPARING AND COOKING — Remove any wilted leaves. Trim stems and cut an X in the bottom of the stem for even cooking. Rinse and soak in lightly salted, cold water 10 minutes if time allows. Cook according to the Paul Mayer Method on page 4. Properly cooked, Brussels sprouts will stay bright green, crunchy and delicious. Serve buttered, sauced or in a recipe.

BRUSSELS SPROUTS SOUFFLE

1-1/4 lbs. Brussels sprouts
1/2 lb. potatoes
3 eggs, separated
1/2 cup (2 oz.) grated Gruyere cheese
6 tbs. soft butter
4 - cup souffle dish

Wash and trim Brussels sprouts. Cook in boiling salted water 15 minutes. Peel and cube potatoes. Cook in small amount of water until very soft. Drain both vegetables well and force through a pureeing device. Add egg yolks, cheese and 4 tablespoons butter to pureed vegetables. Beat egg whites until stiff but not dry. Fold into vegetable mixture. Turn into souffle dish which has been well coated with the remaining 2 tablespoons butter. Bake in 350°F oven 25 minutes or until souffle has puffed and risen.

BRUSSELS SPROUTS IN LEMON SAUCE

1 lb. Brussels sprouts
1/4 cup fresh lemon juice
1/4 cup olive oil
1/2 tsp. salt

50

Trim sprouts and score the bottom of each. Cook by the Paul Mayer Method on page 4. Drain and set over low heat to drive away excess moisture. Combine remaining ingredients in a small bowl. Whisk until creamy. Pour over sprouts. Serve hot. Makes 4 servings.

BRUSSELS SPROUTS IN CREAM CHEESE SAUCE

1-1/2 lbs. Brussels sprouts	1 tsp. lemon juice
1 pkg. (3 oz.) softened cream cheese	1/4 tsp. Worcestershire sauce
1/4 cup sour cream	1/4 tsp. salt
2 tbs. cream	1/4 cup chopped walnuts

Trim and wash Brussels sprouts. Cut an X into the bottom of stem so they will cook evenly. Set aside. Blend cream cheese, sour cream and cream in the top of double boiler. Stir over simmering water until heated. Add lemon juice, Worcestershire and salt. Mixture should be of pouring consistency. Add more cream if needed. Keep sauce warm over water until vegetable is cooked. Cook prepared Brussels sprouts according to the Paul Mayer Method on page 4. Drain well. Place in heated serving dish. Pour hot sauce over Brussels sprouts. Garnish with nuts. Serve immediately. Makes 6 servings.

51

BRUSSELS SPROUTS AND CHESTNUTS

1 lb. chestnuts
2 cups oil
3 tbs. butter
2 tbs. sherry
1 tsp. Bovril
1 tsp. tomato paste
1 tbs. potato flour or cornstarch
1 cup beef stock
1 bay leaf
1 lb. Brussels sprouts

Make a crisscross slash in the flat side of chestnuts. Heat oil to 350°. Drop chestnuts into hot oil and cook 5 minutes. Remove chestnuts. Drain and allow to cool slightly. Remove shells and the skin inside shells. Melt butter in a skillet. Add chestnuts and cook gently until nicely browned. Pour in sherry and ignite. When flame goes out, set pan off heat and remove chestnuts. Add Bovril, tomato

paste and potato flour to skillet. Blend in stock. Return pan to heat. Stir sauce until it boils. Correct seasoning and add bay leaf. Return chestnuts to the pan. Cook very slowly until tender. Trim Brussels sprouts and score the bottom of each one. Cook by the Paul Mayer Method on page 4. Drain and set over low heat to drive away any excess moisture. Combine Brussels sprouts with chestnuts and sauce just before serving. Reheat, and serve in a flat casserole. Makes 4 to 6 servings.

Cauliflower

Cauliflower is native to the Mediterranean area and has been cultivated since at least 600 B.C. England imported it from France in the early 1600s and colonists brought it to America. It is a member of the cabbage family and available the year around. Vitamin C and iron are found in cauliflower.

SELECTING — Look for white, compact heads with fresh appearing leaves. Overmature heads are yellowish and spread open. Cauliflower is usually sold unwrapped and priced by the head. One medium-sized head makes 3 to 4 servings.

STORING — Refrigerate, unwashed, in a plastic bag. Use as soon as possible.

PREPARING AND COOKING — Remove leaves and wash thoroughly. Leave head whole or separate into floweretts, discarding the core. Serve raw as a low calorie snack with dips or cut up in salads, or cook, covered, in as little boiling, salted water as possible. Cook only until barely tender. Depending on size, whole heads take 15 to 25 minutes; flowerets—5 to 9 minutes; smaller pieces—3 to 5 minutes. Drain well and use as desired.

CAULIFLOWER ROMAINE

A nice choice for a luncheon or buffet dish.

1 large cauliflower
2 cups chicken broth
2 large tomatoes
1/4 lb. butter
1 medium onion, finely chopped

1/2 tsp. chervil
1/2 tsp. chives
4 garlic sausages
6 slices white bread

56

Break cauliflower into small flowerettes. Bring chicken broth to boil in saucepan. Add cauliflower and cook 10 minutes. Drain well. Peel, seed and chop tomatoes. Melt 2 tablespoons butter in skillet. Add tomato, onion, chervil and chives. Slice sausages and add to mixture. Cook slowly 25 minutes. Add cauliflower. Transfer mixture to a flat casserole. Bake in 375°F oven 20 to 25 minutes. Melt remaining butter in large skillet. Trim bread and cut into triangles. Fry in hot butter until nicely browned on both sides. Arrange toasted triangles about the casserole and serve at once. Makes 6 servings.

CAULIFLOWER POLONAISE

1 large cauliflower
6 tbs. butter
2 tbs. chopped onion
1 clove garlic
1 tbs. chopped parsley
2 tbs. bread crumbs
1 hard-cooked egg, finely chopped

Divide cauliflower into nice bouquets. Cover with cold salted water. Bring to boil, then simmer gently until barely tender. Drain thoroughly and keep warm. Melt 4 tablespoons butter in the pan in which the cauliflower cooked. Add onions and cook slowly 1 minute. Press garlic and add to onions. Continue cooking slowly a minute or so, or until onion is soft. Add parsley, bread crumbs, egg and remaining butter. Mix with cauliflower and serve. Makes 4 to 6 servings.

CAULIFLOWER FLORENCE-STYLE

Swiss Cheese Sauce, page 59
1 cup cauliflowerets
1-1/2 tbs. butter
3/4 cup chopped mushrooms
1/2 cup green pepper, finely minced
2 tbs. minced onion
8 cooked artichoke bottoms*

58

Prepare sauce as directed. Cook cauliflower just until barely tender. Melt butter in skillet. Saute mushrooms, green pepper and onion until tender. Arrange artichoke bottoms in an ovenproof serving dish. Spoon mushroom mixture onto artichoke bottoms. Top with cauliflowerets. Spoon sauce over all. Run under a heated broiler a few seconds until bubbly. Makes 8 servings.

*Artichoke bottoms may be purchased or prepared fresh as directed on page 19.

SWISS CHEESE SAUCE

2 tbs. butter
2 tbs. flour
3/4 cup light cream or milk
1/2 cup grated Swiss cheese
salt and white pepper to taste
1 tsp. Dijon-style mustard

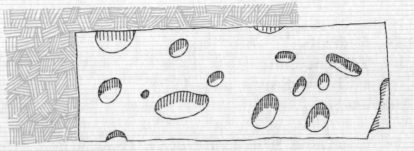

Melt butter in saucepan. Stir in flour and cook 1 minute. Remove from heat. Add cream. Return to heat and cook until mixture thickens and boils. Add salt, pepper and mustard. Keep warm in double boiler over hot water until needed. Press plastic wrap over surface to prevent a crust from forming on top. Use as directed.

CAULIFLOWER PLATTER

1 head cauliflower
4 to 6 carrots
1-1/2 lb. zucchini
Tangy Cheese Sauce, page 11
parsley

Wash and trim cauliflower. Leave whole. Cook in 1-inch boiling, salted water 15 to 20 minutes, or until just tender. Do not overcook. Cut carrots in 1-inch pieces. Cook in boiling salted water just until tender, about 10 minutes. Slice zucchini in 1/2-inch pieces. Cook in small amount of boiling salted water only until barely tender, about 7 minutes. While vegetables are cooking, prepare sauce as directed. To serve, drain vegetables well. Place cauliflower in center of heated serving platter. Alternate servings of zucchini and carrots around it. Spoon sauce over cauliflower. Garnish with parsley. Serve immediately. Makes 6 servings.

CAULIFLOWER WITH CAPERS

An interesting first course, or salad. Even people who think they don't like cauliflower find this tasteful.

1 head cauliflower	salt, pepper, Tabasco
1/2 cup mayonnaise	1 tsp. capers in vinegar*
1 tbs. cream	paprika
1 tbs. lemon juice	

Steam cauliflower whole in 1 inch of boiling, salted water just until tender, about 15 minutes. Drain well. When cool enough to handle, break into flowerets. In large bowl, combine mayonnaise with cream, lemon juice, salt, pepper and Tabasco to taste. Mix well. Add capers. Carefully fold in cauliflowerets. Chill. Serve sprinkled with paprika.

*An important hint—when you open a bottle of capers, pour off its liquid and replace it with white wine vinegar. Let stand several hours or overnight.

Cabbage

Cabbage is one of the most ancient vegetables still grown . . . it may even go back to prehistoric times. Although its origin has not been established, it is known to have been cultivated for over 4,000 years. Cabbage grows in every kind of climate and is readily available all year. It is a good source of vitamin C if not overcooked.

SELECTING — Look for firm, heavy, crisp heads with bright color, whether it is the red or green variety. Allow 1/4 to 1/2 pound per serving.

STORAGE — Refrigerate, unwashed, in a plastic bag. Fresh heads will keep a week or longer.

PREPARING AND COOKING — Rinse and discard outer leaves. Cut in wedges or shred coarsely for cooking. Use a fine shred for cole slaw. Cook rapidly in a small amount of boiling, salted water until tender, but still a bit crisp. Cook 5 to 7 minutes, if shredded; 10 to 15 minutes, for wedges. Avoid overcooking and serve as soon as it is done.

INDONESIAN CURRIED CABBAGE

1 large cabbage
1 large bay leaf
3 whole cloves
1 clove garlic
2 cups beef broth
3 tbs. grated onion

4 tbs. butter
1 tbs. curry powder
6 tbs. flour
salt and cayenne
2 cups milk
1/2 cup grated Gouda cheese

Shred cabbage. Rinse in a colander with lukewarm water. Make a bouquet garni of bay leaf, whole cloves and garlic. Place cabbage, broth and bouquet garni in large kettle. Bring to boil. Cook gently 10 minutes, or until cabbage is tender. Melt butter in another saucepan. Add curry powder and cook gently 1 minute. Remove pan from heat. Stir in flour and season to taste with salt and cayenne. Carefully blend in milk. Return to heat and stir constantly until sauce boils. Drain cabbage well and discard spices. Combine cabbage and sauce. Pour into buttered casserole. Sprinkle with cheese. Bake in 475°F oven 15 minutes, or until top bubbles and is nicely browned. Makes 6 to 8 servings.

CARAWAY CABBAGE

8 cups shredded cabbage
2 eggs, slightly beaten
1 cup half and half
1/2 tsp. salt
pepper to taste
1 tsp. caraway seed.

64   Cut cabbage in 1/4-inch shreds. Cover with ice water. Chill 1 hour. Drain. Cover with lightly salted, boiling water. Simmer 5 minutes. Drain well. Place in buttered, shallow, 2-quart baking dish. Combine eggs, cream, salt, pepper and caraway seeds. Pour over cabbage. Bake in 350°F oven 30 minutes or until custard is set. Makes 6 servings.

HUNGARIAN RED CABBAGE

4 small heads red cabbage
1/2 lb. bacon
1 cup beef stock
1/2 cup red wine vinegar
1/2 cup red wine

2 small green apples, sliced
2 tbs. flour
2 tbs. caraway seeds
sugar

Remove outer leaves and cores from cabbages. Shred cabbage finely. Cook bacon in a large Dutch oven until very crisp. Remove from pan and drain, leaving fat in kettle. Add shredded cabbage and beef stock to hot fat. Cover pan tightly and cook over low heat 1 hour, stirring only occasionally. Heat vinegar to boiling. Add hot vinegar, wine, apple slices and crumbled bacon to cabbage. Season with salt and pepper and cook 15 minutes longer. Remove pot from heat. Thoroughly blend in flour, caraway seeds and enough sugar to give a definite sweet-sour taste. Return to heat and continue cooking until most of the liquid has been absorbed. Serve hot. Makes 6 to 8 servings.

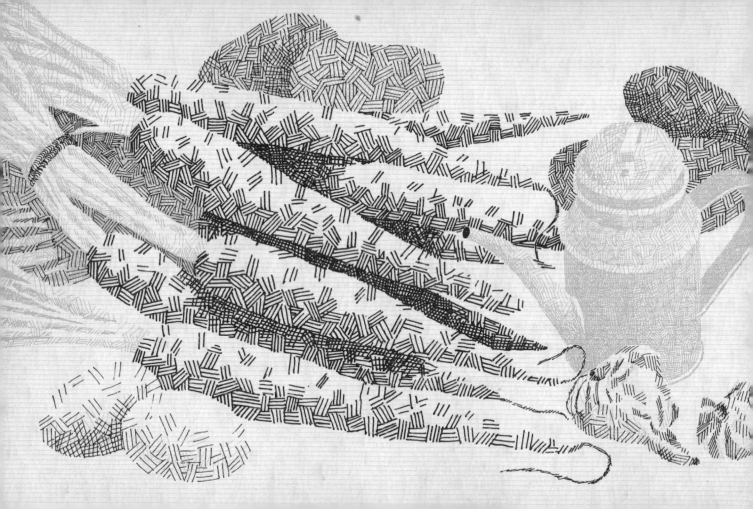

Carrots

Carrots have been around a long time, although their origin is unknown. Ancient Greeks used them for medicine. They were brought by the Dutch to England and to the United States by early colonists. Available all year around, they are an excellent source of vitamin A.

SELECTING — Choose firm, well-shaped, fresh-looking carrots. "Cliptops" are preferred because the tops draw moisture from the carrots. Black stem ends indicate old age. Allow 1 pound for 3 to 4 servings.

STORING — Remove tops if attached. Rinse if freshening is needed. Place in a plastic bag and refrigerate. Will keep up to 2 weeks.

PREPARING AND COOKING — Scrub and peel as thinly as possible. Cook young ones unpeeled. Cut as desired and cook, in as little water as possible over low heat, only until barely tender. Whole baby—8 to 10 minutes; mature ones—10 to 20 minutes; sliced or shredded—4 to 10 minutes.

GLAZED CARROTS

2 bunches carrots
salt
1/4 lb. butter
1/2 cup white sugar
1/2 cup brown sugar
1/2 cup cooking liquid
nutmeg

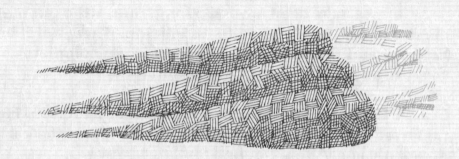

Peel and trim carrots. Cut in half, crosswise. Place in saucepan. Barely cover with cold water. Add a little salt. Bring to boil. Boil gently 3 minutes. Drain well, reserving 1/2 cup cooking liquid. Melt butter in large skillet. Add carrots, sugar and reserved liquid. Sprinkle with a little nutmeg. Cook gently until liquid evaporates and sugar has glazed and browned the carrots nicely. Makes 6 servings.

CARROTS POULETTE

1 bunch carrots
1 cup cooking liquid
1 lemon
3 tbs. butter
3 tbs. flour
salt and cayenne pepper

1/4 cup cream
1 tsp. lemon juice
1 egg yolk
1 tbs. milk
1 tbs. chopped parsley

Peel carrots and cut into pieces. Trim to look like olives by rounding the edges. Cover with salted water and add the juice of the lemon. (Save 1 teaspoon.) Cook until nearly tender, 5 to 10 minutes. Drain and reserve 1 cup of liquid. In the same pan melt 2 tablespoons butter. Remove pan from heat and add flour. Season to taste with salt and cayenne. Blend in the carrot liquid. Stir sauce over medium heat until it boils. Add remaining butter, cream and 1 teaspoon lemon juice. Beat egg yolk into milk. Carefully add to sauce along with parsley. Return carrots to sauce and cook very gently 15 minutes longer. Makes 4 to 6 servings.

CARROTS AND CREAM

2 bunches carrots
2 tbs. butter
1 onion, finely chopped
3 tbs. water
1/4 cup flour
salt and cayenne

1/4 cup milk
1/2 cup whipping cream
2 tbs. cream cheese
1/4 tsp. lemon juice
parsley

Run carrots through the fine blade of a meat grinder or chop by hand until extremely fine. Melt butter in saucepan. Add onion and cook slowly until soft. Add carrots and water. Cover. Cook slowly until carrots are soft and water has cooked away. Do not let carrots brown. Remove from heat and stir in flour. Season with salt and cayenne. Gradually blend in milk and cream. Return to heat. Stir constantly until mixture thickens and boils. Stir in cheese until melted and mixed with carrot puree. Correct seasonings and add 1/4 teaspoon lemon juice. Serve garnished with parsley. Makes 6 servings.

BRANDIED CARROTS

1 lb. carrots
3 tbs. water
4 tbs. butter
salt
2 tbs. brandy
minced parsley

    Peel carrots and cut in thin, diagonal slices. Measure water, 3 tablespoons butter, salt and brandy into saucepan. Add carrots. Cover and cook on low heat until liquid is absorbed and carrots are just tender. Add remaining 1 tablespoon of butter. Heat thoroughly. Serve garnished with parsley. Makes 4 to 6 servings.

BAKED MINTED CARROTS

8 cups carrot slices
1 tsp. salt
1/2 cup brown sugar
6 tbs. butter
1/4 cup chopped fresh mint

72   Place carrots in buttered casserole with cover. Sprinkle with salt and
brown sugar. Dot with butter. Sprinkle with mint. Cover. Bake in 350°F oven 1
hour and 10 minutes. Makes 6 to 8 servings.

VEGETABLE MEDLEY

3 medium carrots
2 stalks celery
1/2 green pepper
1 medium onion, sliced
2 tbs. oil
2 tbs. soy sauce
2 tbs. catsup
2 tbs. water

Pare and slice carrots and celery diagonally. Cut pepper in 1-inch pieces. Separate onion slices into rings. Heat oil. Add vegetables. Cook over medium heat only until onion is partially cooked, about 3 minutes. Add remaining ingredients. Cover and cook over low heat 8 to 10 minutes. Vegetables should remain slightly crisp. Makes 4 servings.

Cucumbers

Cucumbers originated in Asia and go back beyond Old Testament days. Early explorers brought cucumber seeds with them to America and soon the Indians were cultivating them. Still popular today, they are available all year around with Mexico supplementing the supply during our off season.

SELECTING — Look for firm, well-shaped, shiny ones. Avoid those which are puffy, shriveled or have dark sunken spots indicating spoilage. They are usually priced individually. One average-sized cucumber makes 4 servings.

STORING — Refrigerate, wrapped in plastic. Will stay fresh several days.

PREPARING AND COOKING — Wash and leave unpeeled or remove only the very thin skin with a vegetable peeler. Slice and let crisp in lightly salted ice water a few minutes if they are to be served raw. To cook, peel and cut in thick slices. Cook in a small amount of boiling, salted water just until tender, 8 to 10 minutes. Season with butter, salt and pepper.

CUCUMBERS COOKED WITH MINT

This dish goes splendidly with roast lamb.

6 cucumbers
1/4 cup butter
salt and pepper to taste
1-1/2 tsp. chopped fresh mint
1/4 cup cider vinegar

Peel cucumbers and cut them in half lengthwise. With the tip of a spoon, scoop out all of the seeds. Cut cucumber halves into large chunks. Simmer in plenty of boiling, salted water until tender. Drain well and shake over heat to drive out any excess moisture. Remove cucumbers from pot. To the pot add butter, salt and pepper. When butter has melted, add mint and saute about 1 minute. Add cucumbers and toss until hot and well-coated. Add vinegar and bring to boil. Cook until the vinegar has evaporated, leaving behind the mint and butter. Serve at once.

CUCUMBERS IN SOUR CREAM

1 large cucumber
1/2 cup thick sour cream
1-1/2 tbs. cider vinegar
1 tbs. chopped chives
3/4 tsp. salt
1/8 tsp. white pepper
hard-cooked egg yolk

76

Rinse and pare cucumber. Score 1/8 inch deep by drawing tines of a fork lengthwise over entire surface. Cut into thin slices. Combine sour cream, vinegar, chives, salt and pepper. Pour over cucumber slices. Toss lightly to coat evenly. Chill thoroughly. Garnish with finely grated, hard-cooked egg yolk. Makes 4 servings.

DILLED CUCUMBERS ON TOMATO SLICES

1/3 cup salad oil
3 tbs. vinegar
1/2 tsp. _each_ dill weed and salt
1/4 tsp. sugar
1/8 tsp. pepper
1 large cucumber
Bibb lettuce
3 tomatoes, sliced

Measure oil, vinegar, dill weed, salt, sugar and pepper into mixing bowl. Blend with a wire whip. Wash and pare cucumber. Slice paper thin into a shallow dish. Add marinade. Toss to coat. Chill 6 hours or overnight. To serve, arrange lettuce leaves on platter or individual salad plates. Place tomato slices on lettuce. Spoon cucumbers and marinade over tomatoes. Makes 6 servings.

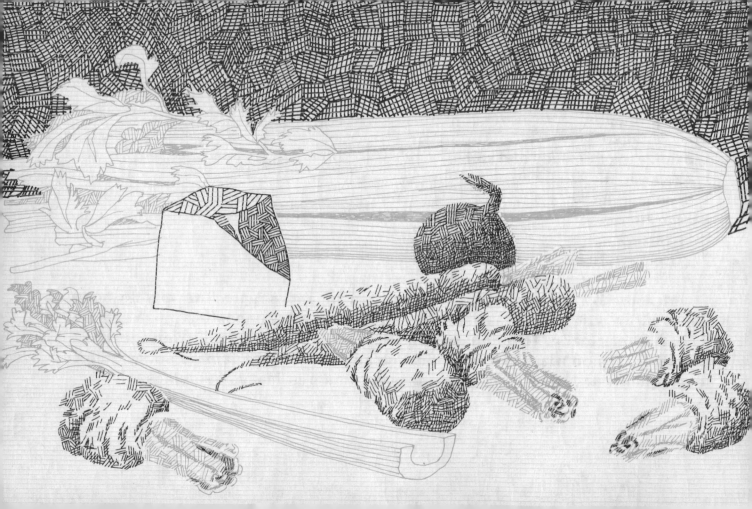

Celery

Celery originated in the Mediterranean area and goes back at least as far as 850 B.C. Seeds were brought to the United States from Scotland in the 1850s and celery became one of our first commercial crops. It is readily available all year and is a good source of sodium and potassium.

SELECTING — Look for well shaped, crisp bunches. Because celery is quite perishable, buy where it is kept on a refrigerated rack. Avoid limp bunches or yellowing leaves. Usually sold and priced by the bunch.

STORING — Trim and rinse. Shake off excess moisture and place in a plastic bag. Close tightly and refrigerate. Will keep up to two weeks.

PREPARING AND COOKING — Separate stalks from bunch. Scrub with a brush and remove strings with a vegetable peeler. Most popular served raw, but also delicious cooked. Cook in as little water or broth as possible. Cover and simmer until barely tender. Serve buttered, combined with other vegetables or prepared in more elaborate ways.

CELERY VICTOR

3 large bunches celery
1-1/2 quarts chicken broth
2 sprigs parsley
1 carrot, sliced
1 onion, sliced
1/2 cup white wine vinegar

1-1/2 cups olive oil
1/2 tsp. chervil
salt and black pepper
flat anchovy fillets
1 can (2 oz.) pimientos
chopped parsley

80

Trim tough outer stalks, roots and most of the leafy tops from celery bunches. Split celery stalks into 3 or 4 pieces each. Bring chicken stock to boil. Add celery, parsley, carrot, onion, and salt to taste. Simmer until celery is barely tender. Drain well. (Refrigerate stock for future use.) Lay drained celery in a flat dish to cool. Mix together vinegar, olive oil, chervil, salt and pepper to taste. Pour this over cooled celery. Refrigerate as long as possible before serving. Crisscross strips of anchovy and pimiento over celery. Sprinkle with chopped parsley. Makes 6 servings.

CELERY ITALIAN-STYLE

6 slices bacon
4 cups sliced celery
1/4 cup chopped onion
1 clove garlic, minced
1 cup water
1 tsp. salt
2 tomatoes, peeled and chopped
1 cup grated Parmesan cheese

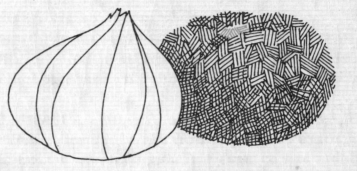

Fry bacon in skillet until crisp. Drain, crumble and set aside. Pour fat from skillet. Add celery, onion, garlic, water and salt. Cover. Simmer 10 minutes or until celery is tender. Drain. Place in 1-1/2 quart casserole. Top with crumbled bacon and chopped tomatoes. Sprinkle with Parmesan. Bake in 350°F oven 15 to 20 minutes. Makes 6 servings.

Celery Root

Celery root is also known as celeriac and is a variety of celery which is grown for its root rather than its tops. If you like celery, you'll love celery root—it's celery, only more so! Popular in Europe, it is almost unknown in many parts of the United States, although it's marketed all year.

SELECTING — Look for celery root with firm, clean roots. Reject any with sprouts coming out on top of the roots as it indicates age. Irregular shapes and dents are natural, but soft spots are a sign of decay. Sold in bulk, by the pound. One pound makes 2 to 3 servings.

STORING — Refrigerate, unwashed, in a plastic bag. Will keep 1 to 2 weeks.

PREPARING AND COOKING — Do not peel or cut celery root until just before cooking as it darkens very quickly when exposed to air. Keep in cold water with a little lemon juice added if it must wait after being peeled or cut. Celery root may be substituted for potatoes in your favorite recipes.

CELERY ROOT AU GRATIN

3 lbs. celery root
salt
1-1/2 cups cooking liquid
1/2 cup butter
6 tbs. flour

cayenne pepper
1 cup (1/2 pt.) whipping cream
2/3 cup grated Parmesan cheese
dry mustard
1/4 cup soft bread crumbs

Peel and dice celery root. Put cubes in water with a little lemon juice added to prevent darkening. When ready to cook, drain and place in saucepan with water to cover and a little salt. Bring to boil. Cook about 20 minutes, or until barely tender. Strain cooking liquid and reserve 1-1/2 cups. Drain cooked celery root very well. Melt 6 tablespoons butter in a saucepan. Remove pan from heat and stir in flour. Add salt and cayenne pepper to taste. Combine cream and reserved liquid. Blend with butter and flour. Return to heat and stir until sauce boils. Add 1/2 cup cheese and a pinch of mustard. Stir over medium heat 2 minutes. Remove from heat and add celery root. Mix well and turn into a large flat casserole. Sprinkle heavily with crumbs, remaining cheese and butter. Bake in 350°F oven 30 minutes. Makes 6 servings.

Eggplant

Eggplants were first cultivated in China and India and carried west by traders. Spanish explorers are credited with bringing them to America where they have been gaining in popularity ever since. They are available in most areas all year with the peak season coming in July and August.

SELECTING — Fresh eggplants are a beautiful deep purple, shiny, firm and heavy for their size. The cap should look fresh and green. These beauties bruise easily and must be handled with care. Avoid those which have dark spots on the surface or look wilted. One medium-sized eggplant will make 4 to 6 servings.

STORING — Eggplants keep better in a cool (50°) place than they do being refrigerated. If such a spot is unavailable, refrigerate only briefly and use as soon as possible after purchasing.

PREPARING AND COOKING — Rinse and dry. Peeling is unnecessary. The way it is cut will depend on how it is to be cooked. Many cultures and cuisines rely heavily on eggplant as a staple vegetable and each one seems to have its own special way of preparing it. I have eaten it throughout Europe and in such unlikely places as Africa and Ceylon. I have met it baked, fried, boiled, broiled, sauteed, breaded, sauced, cooked alone, and combined with meats or other vegetables. It is always delicious and a favorite of mine. To paraphrase Will Rogers, "I've never met an eggplant I didn't like."

86

BAKED STUFFED EGGPLANT

1 large eggplant
3 tbs. butter
1 large onion, finely chopped
1 clove garlic
2 large tomatoes

2 tbs. tomato paste
basil, black pepper
bread crumbs
1/4 cup grated Parmesan cheese
1/4 cup grated Gruyere cheese

Place eggplant in a large pot. Pour boiling water over it. Cover and simmer 15 minutes. Turn eggplant once during this time. Remove from pot and cut in half lengthwise. Scoop out centers and chop. Reserve the shells. Melt butter in another pan. Saute onion until brown. Add garlic through a press and continue cooking 1 minute. Peel, seed and chop tomatoes. Increase heat and add tomatoes. Cook briskly until juice is reduced. Remove pan from heat. Add tomato paste, pinch of basil, salt and pepper to taste. Stir in chopped eggplant and enough dry crumbs to bind the mixture. Spoon into shells and sprinkle the top with more crumbs. Combine Parmesan and Gruyere. Sprinkle over crumbs and dot with butter. Bake in a 450°F oven 10 to 15 minutes or until browned. Makes 6 servings.

EGGPLANT A LA PROVENCALE

2 lbs. tomatoes
1 stalk celery
2 carrots
1 onion
1 tbs. parsley
1/4 cup olive oil
2 cloves garlic
basil, salt, pepper
1/4 cup dry red wine
2 medium eggplants
flour for dredging
1/4 cup butter
2 cups (8 oz.) grated Gruyere cheese

88

Peel, seed and chop tomatoes. Finely chop celery, carrots, onion and parsley. Heat olive oil in saucepan. Add garlic through a press and chopped ingredients. Season to taste with basil, salt and pepper. Cook slowly until thick. Add wine and continue cooking until it thickens again. Set aside. Wash and dry eggplants. Do not peel. Cut into slices. Dredge in flour and shake off excess. Melt butter in large frying pan. Fry eggplant slices in foaming butter until browned on both sides. Place a layer of slices in the bottom of a shallow baking dish. Cover slices with half of the tomato sauce. Cover sauce with half of cheese. Repeat layers. Bake in a hot oven 425°F until cheese is melted and crusts on top, and dish is sizzling hot. Let rest 5 minutes before serving. Makes 6 to 8 servings.

EGGPLANT BAKED WITH ANCHOVIES

3 very small eggplants
salt
1/2 lb. Gruyere cheese, grated
1 can flat anchovies, finely minced
3/4 cup oil

90   Cut eggplants in half lengthwise. Score them deeply with a sharp knife, and sprinkle with salt. Let rest 30 minutes, or until the juices rise and can be wiped away. Mix cheese and anchovies together. After drying the surface of the eggplants, pour 2 tablespoons of oil into the cuts of each half. Spread surfaces with the anchovy-cheese mixture. Place eggplants in a lightly greased baking dish. Bake in a 400°F oven 30 minutes, or until the tops are crusted brown and no longer sticky. Serve at room temperature. Makes 6 servings.

EGGPLANTS FARCIS

3 small eggplants
1 lb. leftover roast beef
1 small onion
4 tbs. butter
salt and black pepper

1/4 cup flour
1 cup whipping cream
Dijon mustard
1/4 lb. Gruyere cheese, grated

Cut the eggplants in half lengthwise. Hollow them out, leaving a shell about 1/4 inch thick. Rub the outside skins of the shell with oil. Chop scooped-out centers. Put roast beef through the fine blade of the meat grinder. Grind onion and then grind beef a second time. Melt butter in a skillet. Add meat, chopped eggplant, salt and pepper. Cook slowly until meat is heated through and eggplant is cooked. Remove from heat. Add flour and blend in cream. Continue cooking until cream thickens and the hash is firm. Correct seasoning and add mustard to taste. Fill reserved shells with mixture. Sprinkle tops with cheese. Bake in a 400°F oven until crusted and browned, and the skins themselves are soft. Serve hot. Makes 6 servings.

EGGPLANT TORTA

1 large eggplant
seasoned flour
peanut oil
salt, pepper, thyme to taste
1/2 cup chopped parsley
1 onion, finely chopped
2 green peppers, finely chopped
6 large tomatoes
2 pkg (8 oz. ea.) sliced Mozzarella cheese
1 cup (1/2 pt.) whipping cream
1/2 cup half and half
3 eggs
2 egg yolks
nutmeg

Peel and slice eggplant. Dredge in seasoned flour. Fry in hot, deep oil until nicely browned and soft. Place half the eggplant slices in a large oblong baking dish. Season with salt, pepper, thyme and 2 tablespoons chopped parsley. Peel, seed and slice tomatoes. Cover eggplant slices with half the tomatoes. Sprinkle tomatoes with salt, pepper, more parsley, half the onion and half the peppers. Cover with half the cheese slices. Repeat layers ending with cheese. Beat remaining ingredients together. Pour over layered ingredients. Bake in 425°F oven 30 to 40 minutes or until the custard is completely set and cheese is deeply browned. Remove from oven. Let rest 5 minutes before serving. Makes 6 servings.

EGGPLANT CANNELONI

1 cup grated Mozzarella cheese
1/2 cup grated Parmesan cheese
1/3 cup ricotta cheese
2 eggs
1/4 cup chopped parsley
1 tbs. chopped ham
salt and pepper
1 egg white, stiffly beaten
2 tbs. flour
1/2 tsp. baking powder
1/3 cup milk
1 tbs. salad oil
2 eggplants
flour for dredging
1/4 cup olive oil
2 tbs. butter
Tomato Sauce, page 96

In a mixing bowl combine Mozzarella, Parmesan, ricotta, 1 egg, 1 tablespoon parsley, ham, salt and pepper to taste. Blend to a smooth paste. Fold in stiffly beaten egg white. Chill mixture thoroughly. In another bowl sift together flour, baking powder and 1/2 teaspoon salt. Add remaining egg, milk and salad oil. Beat until smooth. Peel eggplants. Cut in half lengthwise. Starting from cut surfaces, shave three thin slices from each of the four halves, yielding 12 thin, wide pieces. Dredge slices in flour and shake off excess. Heat olive oil and butter together. Dip eggplant slices in prepared batter until they are evenly, but thinly, coated. Saute in hot oil and butter mixture until browned on both sides. Drain slices well on paper towels. Place about 2 tablespoons of the chilled cheese mixture on each slice. Roll up loosely. Arrange rolls, seam side down, on a lightly buttered baking pan. Cover with Tomato Sauce. Bake in a moderately hot 375°F oven 15 minutes, or until cheese melts, eggplant is thoroughly heated and the sauce is sizzling. Sprinkle with finely chopped parsley and serve immediately. Makes 6 servings.

TOMATO SAUCE

2 tbs. butter
3 tbs. flour
1 cup stewed tomatoes
1 can (6 oz.) tomato paste
pinch sugar
salt, black pepper to taste
1 clove garlic, pressed

96

Melt butter in saucepan. Remove from heat and stir in flour. Blend in tomatoes, tomato paste, sugar, salt, pepper and garlic. Return to heat and stir until mixture boils. Use as directed.

FRENCH FRIED EGGPLANT

1 large eggplant
3 eggs
1 tsp. water
flour
dry bread crumbs
salt and black pepper
2 cloves garlic
fat for French frying

Peel eggplant. Beat eggs with water in a pie plate. Put flour in a similar plate. Combine bread crumbs, salt, black pepper and pressed garlic in a paper bag. Cut eggplant into 1/2 inch slices. Cut slices into half-inch strips as for French fried potatoes. Dredge strips in flour. Dust off any excess. Dip in beaten egg and drop into the bag. Shake the bag to thoroughly coat eggplant strips. Shake off excess crumbs and allow to dry 15 minutes. Fry a few strips at a time in hot (350°) fat, until browned. Drain on absorbent paper and serve. Makes 4 to 6 servings.

Green Beans

Green beans originated in the Americas and have long been a favorite. Grown mostly in California and Florida they are available fresh the year around. The peak season comes in mid- to late summer. Green beans are a good source of vitamins A and C with a trace of calcium.

SELECTING — Look for crisp, bright green beans that are not too full. Young ones have a velvety feel. Avoid wilted, bruised or broken beans. Usually sold loose and priced by the pound. Allow 1/4 pound per serving.

STORING — Refrigerate, unwashed, in a plastic bag. Use as soon as possible.

PREPARING AND COOKING — Rinse well. Snap off both tips and break or cut into pieces, cut French-style or leave whole. Cook according to the Paul Mayer Method on page 4. Cooked this way, green beans stay sweet, bright and delicious.

GREEN BEANS VINAIGRETTE IN TOMATOES

2 to 3 tbs. Kosher-style dill pickle pieces
2 to 3 tbs. <u>each</u> chives and capers
1 cup olive oil
1/2 cup tarragon vinegar
salt and pepper to taste
pinch dry mustard, paprika
1-1/2 lbs. green beans
6 large tomatoes
lettuce leaves
parsley sprigs

Remove seeds from pickles. Finely chop pickle pieces, chives and capers. Blend together oil, vinegar, salt, pepper, mustard and paprika. Add chopped pickles, chives and capers. Refrigerate until needed. Wash beans and slice on a French slicer. Cook according to the Paul Mayer Method on page 4. Drain and rinse with cold water. When well drained and cooled, place in a bowl and add vinaigrette dressing. Mix well and refrigerate several hours or overnight. A few hours before serving time, dip tomatoes in boiling water for 15 seconds. Immediately plunge into cold water. Slip off skins. Hollow out centers removing core, seeds and some pulp from each one. Chill. At serving time, dry the inside of each tomato and fill with marinated beans. Arrange lettuce leaves on 6 salad plates. Place tomatoes on lettuce and garnish with parsley sprigs. Makes 6 servings.

101

GREEN BEANS ITALIAN-STYLE

4 very ripe tomatoes
2 lbs. green beans
3 tbs. olive oil
1 large onion, finely minced

1 large clove garlic
4 tbs. tomato paste
salt, black pepper, basil
1 tsp. sugar

102   Peel tomatoes and cut into quarters. Wash beans and put through a French slicer. Cook sliced beans by the Paul Mayer Method on page 4. Drain well. Heat olive oil in a large skillet. Add onion and garlic (through a press). Cook slowly until onion is soft. Increase heat and add tomatoes, tomato paste, salt, pepper, sugar, and a good deal of crushed basil to taste. Continue cooking over high heat until tomatoes are completely reduced, and enough liquid has cooked away to give a fairly thick consistency. Add beans, and reheat in the sauce only long enough to make sure they are hot. Do not continue cooking beans in hot sauce or they will loose their color and crispness. Makes 6 servings.

GREEN BEANS A LA POULETTE

3/4 lb. white beans
2 lbs. green beans
4 tbs. butter
2 tsp. flour
3/4 cup reserved liquid

freshly ground pepper
6 tbs. whipping cream
1 egg yolk
1-1/2 tbs. lemon juice
1 tbs. chopped parsley

Soak beans several hours. Drain. Cover with salted water. Bring to boil then simmer 1-1/2 hours or until tender. Cut green beans into pieces. Cook according to the Paul Mayer Method on page 4. Drain and reserve 3/4 cup liquid. Melt butter in saucepan. Stir in flour. Cook slowly 3 to 4 minutes without letting flour color. Slowly stir in liquid. Simmer 10 minutes. Season with pepper. Combine cream and egg yolk. Add a little hot sauce to cream mixture, then stir back into sauce. Heat, but do not boil. Add lemon juice. Divide sauce equally. Add drained white beans to one part of sauce. Combine green beans, remaining sauce and parsley. Place white beans in the center of serving platter. Arrange green beans around white beans. Serve immediately. Makes 6 to 8 servings.

GREEN BEANS NICOISE

2-1/2 lbs. green beans
1 cup butter
1 lb. tomatoes
1 clove garlic
2 oz. anchovies, mashed
chopped parsley

104 Wash beans and put through a French slicer. (A small tool readily available in housewares departments.) Cook beans according to the Paul Mayer Method on page 4. Drain thoroughly. Melt 7 tablespoons butter in large saucepan. Add beans and saute gently 5 minutes. Peel, seed and chop tomatoes. Melt remaining butter in skillet. Add tomatoes, garlic through a press and anchovies. Cook briskly until liquid has all cooked away. Combine beans and tomato mixture. Transfer to well-buttered, ovenproof serving dish. Bake in 350°F oven 5 to 10 minutes or until thoroughly heated. Sprinkle with parsley and serve. Makes 6 servings.

GREEN BEANS AND MUSHROOMS IN CREAM

2 lbs. green beans
1/4 cup butter
1/2 lb. mushrooms, thinly sliced
1 cup (1/2 pt.) whipping cream
1/2 cup sour cream
salt, pepper and basil

Put beans through a French slicer. Cook them by the Paul Mayer Method on page 4 and drain thoroughly. Melt butter in a large skillet. When just beginning to brown, add mushrooms, a few at a time. Keep heat high. Cook until crisply browned. Add whipping cream and sour cream and continue cooking until creams have cooked away and the mushrooms are coated. Add beans and seasonings. Mix quickly together to reheat beans and serve. Makes 6 servings.

SWISS BEANS

1-1/2 lbs. green beans
2 tbs. butter
2 tbs. flour
1 tsp. sugar
1/4 tsp. pepper

1/2 tsp. grated onion
1 cup sour cream
1/2 lb. Swiss cheese, grated
2 cups corn flakes
2 tbs. melted butter

Rinse beans and snap off tips. Break each bean into 3 or 4 pieces. Cook according to the Paul Mayer Method on page 4. Drain well. Melt butter in saucepan. Stir in flour, sugar, pepper and onion. Cook 2 minutes. Reduce heat. Add sour cream. Stir until smooth. Fold in beans and heat gently. Turn into buttered casserole. Sprinkle with cheese. Mix corn flakes and butter. Scatter over cheese. Bake in 400°F oven 20 minutes or until bubbly and crumbs are nicely browned. Makes 8 servings.

GREEN BEANS EN CASSEROLE

2 lbs. green beans
1 can (5 oz.) water chestnuts
1 lb. mushrooms, sliced
1 onion, chopped
1/2 cup (1/4 lb.) butter
1/4 cup flour
2 cups milk

1 cup (1/2 pt.) cream
3/4 lb. sharp cheddar, grated
1/8 tsp. Tabasco sauce
2 tsp. soy sauce
1 tsp. salt
1/2 tsp. pepper
1/2 cup toasted slivered almonds

Rinse beans and snap off ends. Break each bean into about 3 pieces. Cook according to the Paul Mayer Method on page 4. Drain well. Drain and slice chestnuts. Melt butter in large saucepan. Saute mushrooms and onions about 5 minutes. Stir in flour and cook 1 minute. Remove from heat. Slowly blend in milk and cream. Return to heat. Cook, stirring, until mixture thickens and boils. Add cheese, Tabasco, soy, salt and pepper. Add beans and chestnuts to sauce. Turn into buttered casserole. Sprinkle with almonds. Bake in 375°F oven 20 minutes or until bubbly. Makes 8 servings.

Green Peppers

Big sweet peppers, called "bell" because of their shape, can be either red or green depending on when they are harvested. The red ones have been allowed to ripen fully before being picked. Peak season for green peppers is August and September, with red ones coming later in the fall. Peppers are high in vitamins A and C, and also contain calcium, phosphorous, iron, sodium, magnesium, thiamin, riboflavin and niacin and are very low in calories.

108

SELECTING — Look for firm, shiny, dark green peppers. Immature ones are pale while older ones will be dull and probably shriveled. Check stems for decay and watch for black spots caused by the rain. For stuffing, buy well-shaped peppers which will stand level. Allow 1/2 to 1 pepper per serving.

STORING — Refrigerate, unwashed and unwrapped in crisper.

PREPARING AND COOKING — Wash. If stuffing, slice off top, or cut in half lengthwise. Parboil if recipe specifies. Peppers freeze beautifully. Simply chop and place on a flat surface. Freeze, then transfer to containers.

STUFFED GREEN PEPPERS GALLIA PALACE

6 large green peppers
1 loaf (1 lb.) firm white bread
milk
2 cups cooked chicken breast, ground
1/2 cup pine nuts
1/2 cup light raisins
1 large egg, well beaten
salt and white pepper

Wash peppers. Slice off tops and remove seeds. Rinse insides and drain. Remove crusts from bread slices. Reduce to crumbs using blender or fingers. Add enough milk to crumbs to thoroughly moisten. Add remaining ingredients. Mix well and pack into peppers. Replace tops. Stand peppers in shallow baking dish with about 1 inch of stock or water. Bake in 350°F oven about 30 minutes or until peppers are thoroughly cooked. Cool and serve at room temperature. Makes 6 servings.

GREEN AND RED PEPPERS PROVENCALE

2 cloves garlic
1/2 cup olive oil
3 tbs. tarragon vinegar
1 tbs. <u>each</u> finely chopped parsley,
    tarragon, chervil and chives*
salt and pepper to taste
2 large green peppers
2 large red bell peppers
3 large firm ripe tomatoes
6 hard-cooked eggs
anchovies
pitted ripe olives

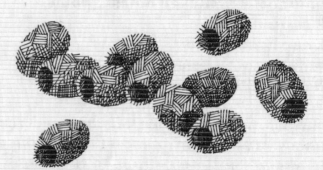

110

Put garlic through a press into small mixing bowl. Add olive oil, vinegar, finely chopped herbs, salt and pepper. Mix together well. Wash and dry peppers. Place peppers in a 400°F oven until skins puff, about 10 to 12 minutes.

Wash off loosened skin under running water. Cut peppers into finger lengths. Remove seeds and membranes. Peel and slice tomatoes and eggs. Place tomato slices on the bottom of a large flat serving dish. Spoon 1/4 of the dressing over tomatoes. Add a layer of green pepper slices and a little more dressing. Add red pepper slices next and more dressing. Cover red peppers with egg slices. Pour remaining dressing over eggs. Decorate with a lattice work of anchovy slices. Place an olive in the center of each diamond. Chill as long as possible before serving. Makes 8 servings.

*If substituting dried herbs for fresh ones, use 1/2 teaspoon of each.

Mushrooms

Mushrooms are a fungus which has been around for hundreds of thousands of years, but was first cultivated in France in the 1700s. Commercial cultivation was started in the United States in 1890. Controlled growing keeps their price fairly stable all year. They are sold loose and by the pound.

SELECTING — Buy mushrooms with closed caps. If the cap is open and the dark fluting under it is exposed, the mushrooms may have lost some of their moisture. They should look fresh and be without bruises. Size has nothing to do with age or flavor. Choose the size which best suits your need.

STORING — Store spread out, covered with damp paper towels or in a plastic bag left open to allow air to circulate. Refrigerate. Will keep a week or so.

PREPARING AND COOKING — Never soak or peel. Simply wipe mushrooms with a damp towel and trim off stem end. Use raw or saute briefly in butter.

113

MUSHROOMS WITH CRAB LEGS

24 large mushrooms
1/4 lb. butter
24 whole crab legs
6 tbs. flour
salt and white pepper
1-1/2 cups milk
2 tbs. grated onion
Tabasco sauce
1 tsp. Dijon mustard
3/4 cup grated Parmesan cheese
1 cup (1/2 pt.) whipping cream
2 egg yolks
1/4 cup dry bread crumbs

114

Wash mushrooms. Dry and remove stems. Melt 4 tablespoons butter. Dip mushrooms in butter and arrange on a lightly greased cookie sheet. Place crab leg in each mushroom cap. Melt remaining butter in saucepan. Remove from heat and stir in flour, salt and pepper to taste. Blend milk in gradually. Add onion, Tabasco and mustard. Return to heat and stir until mixture boils. Add 1/2 cup Parmesan. Continue boiling until the cheese melts. Add only enough cream to give the sauce a smooth, but slightly heavy consistency. Beat egg yolks. To them add a little of the hot sauce, then quickly stir mixture back into sauce. Do not let sauce boil after adding the yolks. Coat mushrooms and crab legs with sauce. Sprinkle with remaining cheese and bread crumbs which have been combined. Bake in 475°F oven 10 minutes, or until browned. Makes 12 servings.

MUSHROOMS AND SOUR CREAM

2 lbs. mushrooms
1/4 lb. butter
2 tbs. Worcestershire sauce
salt and black pepper
2 cups (1 pt.) sour cream
toast points

116

Wash mushrooms. Trim stems and slice thinly. Heat butter in a large heavy skillet until it just begins to brown. Add mushrooms, a few at a time. Keep heat high. Continue cooking, stirring as little as possible, until mushrooms are nicely browned. Add Worcestershire, salt and pepper to taste. Stir in sour cream and continue cooking on high heat. Stir occasionally to prevent scorching. When sour cream has cooked away and mushrooms are coated, the dish is done. Serve it hot over toast for brunch or as an accompaniment for steaks. Makes 6 servings.

MUSHROOMS WITH GARLIC AND HERBS

1/4 tsp. <u>each</u> turmeric, cumin,
    coriander, ginger
1/2 tsp. each rosemary, thyme, basil
1/4 lb. butter
4 shallots, finely chopped
1 lb. button mushrooms
salt and pepper

1/2 cup (4 oz.) brandy
3 cloves garlic
1 tbs. chopped parsley
pinch cayenne
1 tsp. potato flour or cornstarch
3 cups whipping cream

Mix spices and herbs together and pulverize. Set aside. Melt butter in large skillet. Add shallots and mushrooms. Cook 2 minutes. Season with salt and pepper. Pour in brandy and ignite. When flame dies out, add garlic through a press, parsley, the pulverized seasonings and a pinch of cayenne pepper. Stir in potato flour. Carefully blend in cream and stir until mixture boils. Reduce heat and cook until sauce thickens and reaches a nice creamy consistency. Serve in small ramekins. Sprinkle with remaining parsley. Makes 6 servings.

MUSHROOMS WITH GREEN BEANS

2 lbs. green beans
1/2 cup butter
1/2 lb. mushrooms, thinly sliced
salt, pepper and basil

Put beans through a French slicer. Cook them by the Paul Mayer Method on page 4 and drain thoroughly. Melt 4 tablespoons butter in a large skillet. When it is just beginning to turn brown, add sliced mushrooms, a few at a time. Keep the heat high. Cook until crisply browned. add beans and remaining butter. Season with salt, pepper and a pinch of basil. Serve hot. Makes 6 servings.

118

MUSHROOMS STUFFED WITH SPINACH

24 giant mushrooms
1/4 lb. plus 3 tbs. butter
3 bunches spinach
2 large onions, finely chopped
1 tsp. Bovril

1/4 cup flour
3/4 cup beef stock
salt and black pepper
1/4 cup grated Gruyere
1/4 cup grated Parmesan

Remove stems and wash mushrooms. Pat dry. Saute quickly in 1/4 pound very hot butter. Do not overcook. Place in shallow baking pan. Thoroughly wash spinach several times. Cook quickly over high heat, using only the water that clings to the leaves. Squeeze small handfuls of cooked spinach until completely moisture free. Force dry spinach through the fine blade of a meat grinder. Set aside. In a large, heavy skillet melt remaining butter. Add onions and cook until browned. Remove pan from heat and stir in Bovril and flour. Blend in beef stock and season to taste with salt and pepper. Stir over medium heat until mixture boils and becomes very thick. Stir in spinach. Stuff mushrooms with spinach mixture. Combine Gruyere and Parmesan and sprinkle over spinach. Bake in 425°F oven until tops are browned. Makes 6 to 8 servings.

Onions

Onions originated in Asia and go back to prehistoric times. Spaniards brought them to North America, and now billions of pounds are grown in the United States each year. Green onions are small onion plants harvested when the bulbs are 1/4 to 1/2 inch in diameter. If left they become dry onions.

SELECTING — Choose firm dry onions. The outer paper-dry skin should look bright and smooth. Check the stem for softness or sprouts which indicate old age. Green onions should have crisp tops. They are always priced by the bunch, while dry ones are sold loose by the pound or in cello bags.

STORING — Keep dry onions in cool dry place away from potatoes because they give off moisture which causes onions to sprout and rot.

PREPARING AND COOKING — Remove only the paper thin skin from dry onions. Slice, chop or leave whole. Onions are used in endless ways with almost every kind of food. Green ones are most popular served raw.

ONIONS BLAZED WITH CURACAO

Small white onions usually end up either in stews or boiled. Here is a switch, to enhance the menu the next time duck with orange sauce is served.

24 small boiling onions
1/4 lb. plus 2 tbs. butter
3 tbs. Curacao, Cointreau or Triple Sec

122

Peel onions and make crisscross cuts in tops and bottoms so the centers will not jump out during cooking. Cook 5 to 7 minutes in plenty of boiling, salted water. Drain well. Melt butter in a skillet. Saute onions until nicely browned, moving them around carefully so they color evenly all over. Just before serving, pour liqueur over onions. Ignite and serve blazing if possible. Makes 6 servings.

CREAMED PEARL ONIONS

2 lbs. tiny boiling onions
2 tbs. butter
2 tbs. flour
1/4 tsp. salt
1/8 tsp. white pepper
1 cup light cream

Pour boiling water over onions. Let stand 2 to 3 minutes. Drain and peel. 123
Make an X in the root end of each onion to help keep them intact while cooking. Drop peeled onions into boiling, salted water to cover. Cook, uncovered,
just until tender, about 12 to 15 minutes. Drain and set aside. Melt butter in
saucepan. Blend in flour and seasonings. Stir until bubbly. Remove from heat.
Add cream. Return to heat. Cook, stirring, until mixture thickens and boils 1
minute. Add drained onions to sauce. Makes 6 servings.

ONIONS A LA PARMESAN

8 medium onions, sliced
1/4 cup butter
1/2 cup grated Parmesan cheese

Saute onion slices in butter 10 to 12 minutes. Remove to baking dish. Sprinkle cheese over top. Broil 5 inches from heat until cheese melts. Makes 6 servings.

124

Leeks

Leeks were known in Egypt and other Mediterranean countries before Biblical times. By 640 A.D. they had reached Wales and eventually were brought to America by the colonists. Available all year with peak months from September to November and in May.

SELECTING — Look for leeks that have several inches of white, are not too big, and are well shaped with fresh green tops.

125

STORING — Wash, dry and refrigerate in a plastic bag. Use right away.

PREPARING AND COOKING — Leeks require drastic trimming. Cut off root ends. Trim away all but about 1-1/4 inches of green. Remove tough outside leaves. Wash thoroughly to be sure no sand lurks within the layers. Cut in half lengthwise or leave whole and boil or braise. Slice and use in soup, stews or serve in a sauce. Also good used raw in salads.

BRAISED LEEKS SCOTCH STYLE

This robust presentation is especially good with baked ham.

24 small leeks
2 tbs. <u>each</u> finely chopped carrots, onions,
    parsley, celery leaves, green peper
salt and black pepper
nutmeg, thyme, basil
2 cups hot beef stock
buttered paper
2 tbs. butter
1/4 cup flour
1-1/2 cups half & half
cayenne pepper
3 egg yolks, beaten
1/2 cup soft, buttered bread crumbs

Trim leeks and thoroughly wash in lukewarm water. Rinse in several changes of cold water. Drain and dry. Arrange leeks in a buttered, shallow baking dish. Spread chopped vegetables over them. Season with salt, pepper, nutmeg, thyme and basil. Barely cover with hot stock. Cover the dish with buttered paper. Bake in 375°F oven 40 minutes, or until leeks are tender. Thoroughly drain off all liquid and refrigerate for future use. Melt butter in saucepan. Remove from heat and stir in flour. Add cream, salt and cayenne to taste. Stir over medium heat until sauce boils. Add a little of the hot sauce to beaten egg yolks. Then beat mixture back into the hot sauce. Pour over leeks and sprinkle with bread crumbs. Return to oven for 20 minutes, or until sauce is browned. Makes 6 servings.

Potatoes

What can anyone say about potatoes that hasn't already been said and cannot be repeated in two words—"they're great"?

Potatoes were first cultivated in Chile and in their case the process was reversed ... Spanish explorers took them from the Americas to Europe. They were resisted in many parts but the cultivation of potatoes in Europe finally had its start in Ireland about 1565. Now they are available practically everywhere, the year around.

SELECTING — When buying potatoes, choose wisely and choose the variety best suited to your purpose. Idahoes are indeed best for baking, but there it stops. White Rose, Shafters or large red skins are best for boiling, mashing, salads and frying. While the tiny pink skinned ones make splendid salad also, they are really best served whole, hot and in their skins. Regardless of the kind of potato you are buying, look for well-shaped, firm ones of fairly uniform size. Avoid those with sprouts, green spots or a greenish cast which indicates long storage or over-exposure to light. They are apt to have a bitter taste.

STORAGE — Keep in a cool, dry, dark place. Never refrigerate potatoes. Properly stored, potatoes will keep two or three weeks.

PREPARING AND COOKING — Potatoes can be peeled, or scrubbed and cooked in their skins. The kind of potatoes and the way they are to be used determines how they should be cooked.

As you have probably guessed, I love potatoes and am constantly exploring new ways of presenting this fascinating vegetable. Perhaps that is why this section is somewhat fatter than the others!

AU GRATIN POTATOES

8 tbs. butter
6 potatoes
salt and pepper
3 tsp. flour
2 cups (8 oz.) sharp cheddar cheese, grated
2 cups milk, scalded

Spread 2 tablespoons butter over the bottom of a flat, ovenproof dish. Peel and slice potatoes. Put in a pot and add enough boiling water to cover. Boil 3 minutes. Drain well. Place a layer of potatoes in buttered dish. Sprinkle with salt and pepper and 1 teaspoon flour. Dot with 2 tablespoons butter and cover with 1/2 cup cheese. Repeat layers twice more, ending with cheese on top. Pour milk over layers and bake in 350°F oven 40 to 45 minutes or until the top is golden. Serve at once. Makes 6 servings.

GARLIC POTATOES

4 large pink potatoes
6 tbs. butter
3 cloves garlic
salt and black pepper

Peel potatoes. Gently boil in salted water until barely tender. Drain. Put drained potatoes back into pan and shake over heat until they appear to have flour on the outside. Cool and thinly slice. Melt butter in large skillet. Add garlic through a press. Season with salt and pepper. Add potatoes to skillet. Turn them about in the butter then press together to form a large flat cake. Cook over a slow heat. Turn the whole mass with a spatula fairly frequently until a nice brown crust has formed. Serve hot. Makes 6 servings.

POTATOES A LA DAUPHINOISE

2 lbs. potatoes
5 tbs. butter
2 cups grated Gruyere cheese
salt and white pepper
1 cup (1/2 pt.) whipping cream

Peel and thinly slice potatoes. Butter a baking dish lightly, then dot the bottom of dish with 1 tablespoon butter. Barely cover with a little grated cheese. Sprinkle with salt and pepper. Place half of potato slices on top of cheese and season again. Scatter half of remaining cheese on top of potatoes. Dot liberally with 2 tablespoons butter. Layer on remaining potatoes and cheese. Season and dot with remaining butter. Pour cream over top. Bake in 425°F oven 45 minutes to 1 hour, or until potatoes are soft but crisp on top. Makes 6 servings.

POTATO DUMPLINGS

5 medium-sized potatoes
1-1/2 cups fine fresh bread crumbs
2 tsp. grated onion
2 beaten eggs
1 tbs. flour
salt and pepper
3 qts. boiling salted water

134

Grate potatoes and squeeze absolutely dry. Mix with crumbs, onion, eggs, flour and seasonings. Dip fingers into flour and shape mixture into balls the size of walnuts. Lightly flour and drop into boiling water. Cover pot tightly and boil 15 minutes. Remove from water with a slotted spoon. Drain on absorbent paper before serving. Makes 4 to 6 servings.

POTATOES AND CELERY ROOT AU GRATIN

3 large red potatoes
1 large or 2 small celery roots
8 tbs. butter
2 tbs. potato flour or cornstarch
salt and cayenne pepper

1-1/2 cups milk
1-1/2 cups whipping cream
1-1/2 cups grated Parmesan cheese
1 cup grated Gruyere cheese
1/4 tsp dry mustard

Peel potatoes and celery root. Cut into medium-sized dice. In Dutch oven melt 6 tablespoons butter. Add potatoes and celery root. Saute until they begin to crisp and brown. Remove from heat and stir in potato flour. Season to taste. Heat milk and cream together and carefully blend into saucepan mixture. Return to heat. Stir until mixture boils. Add 1 cup Parmesan and all of Gruyere. Continue stirring gently until cheese melts and blends into the sauce. Turn mixture into a large flat ovenproof dish which has been well-buttered. Sprinkle with remaining Parmesan and dot with butter. Bake in 450°F oven 10 to 15 minutes, or until the top is bubbling, crusted and nicely browned. Makes 6 servings.

DUCHESSE POTATOES

Serve as rich mashed potatoes or pipe through a pastry tube for garnishing a planked steak or Fillet of Sole Marguery.

2 lbs. potatoes
2 tbs. butter
1 tsp. salt
2 eggs
136 2 egg yolks

Peel potatoes and cut into pieces. Cook in boiling salted water until soft. Drain well. Briefly shake pan over low heat to drive off excess moisture. Place in large mixer bowl. Beat until smooth. Add butter and salt. Beat well. Add eggs and yolks one at a time. Beat well after each addition. Makes 8 servings.

POTATOES LORETTE

A delicious combination of Duchesse Potatoes and unbaked cream puff pastry—pate a choux—deep fried to golden perfection.

Duchesse Potatoes, page 136
1 cup water
2 tbs. butter
1/2 tsp. salt

dash cayenne
1 cup flour
4 eggs
deep hot fat

Prepare Duchesse Potatoes and set aside. Put water, butter, salt and cayenne in saucepan. Bring to boil and add flour all at once. Turn heat off but keep pot on burner while beating in flour until smooth and shiny, and mixture leaves the sides of the pan. Transfer to large mixer bowl. Beat in eggs, one at a time. Blend in Duchesse Potatoes. Drop by spoonfuls into hot (350°F) fat. Cook until puffed and browned. Drain on absorbent paper. Makes 6 to 8 servings.

POTATO BASKETS

6 large potatoes*
hot (350°-380°) deep fat

Peel and shred potatoes. Keep in cold water until needed, then drain well and squeeze as dry as possible. Using a basket-making tool, pack enough potatoes into the tool to make a fairly thick basket. Then use the smaller half of the tool to form the basket shape and hold it. Lower the contrivance into the hot fat. Fry until both the inside and outside of the potato basket are deep brown and crisp. Remove from fat and very carefully knock the basket loose without tearing it. When potatoes are not thoroughly cooked, they will stick to the tool. If this happens, fry a little longer.

*Do not use Idahos.

POTATO CREPES

1-1/2 lbs. potatoes
1 onion
salt and pepper
nutmeg
5 eggs
butter

Peel potatoes and onion and cut into pieces. Place in blender container with seasonings. Cover and blend on high speed until potatoes are grated and well mixed with the seasonings. Drain well, but do not squeeze dry. Beat in eggs, one at a time. Do not use blender for adding eggs. Melt a small amount of butter in a crepe pan. Cook potato crepes the same as any crepes. Sprinkle with more seasoning and serve immediately. Makes 6 servings.

Note: Do not make ahead as the potatoes will darken and the pancakes will become soft and soggy if they stand too long before being used.

POTATO PANCAKES

6 potatoes
2 eggs
1-1/2 tbs. flour
1/4 tsp. baking powder
1-1/4 tsp. salt
1 small onion, grated
1 lb. lard

141

Grate potatoes into a large mixing bowl. Beat eggs and add to potatoes. Sift dry ingredients together. Add to potatoes. Stir in onion. Melt enough lard in a large skillet to give a depth of 1/2 inch. When it is smoking hot, drop in batter by spoonsful. Cook until crisp on both sides. Serve at once. Makes 6 servings.

POTATOES SALARDAISE

Small oval casserole with a tight fitting lid is absolutely essential for this recipe.

2 potatoes
3 truffles
3 tbs. butter
salt and black pepper
flour and water

Peel potatoes. Slice potatoes and truffles as thinly as possible. Place butter in bottom of casserole. Add potatoes and truffles and mix together well. Season with salt and pepper. Place lid on casserole. Make a stiff paste of flour and water. Use to SEAL the lid onto the casserole. Bake in 325°F oven 1 hour if you want the potatoes to be very brown, or about 40 minutes if you prefer them softer. Don't crack the seal until the potatoes reach the table. Makes 4 servings.

HOT POTATO CHIPS

3 large potatoes
ice water
hot deep fat

Peel potatoes. Using a mechanical slicer, slice as thinly as possible. Soak in ice water. Just before cooking, drain slices and dry thoroughly with paper towelling or a cloth towel. Heat fat to 350°F. Fry a few slices at a time until golden brown and crisp. Drain. Sprinkle with salt and serve. Makes 6 servings.

ROSTI

4 large potatoes
6 tbs. butter
2 cups chicken broth
salt and black pepper

144

Grate potatoes on the side of the grater with the largest opening so they come out shredded rather than finely grated. Melt butter in a heavy skillet. Pack potatoes into skillet after turning them once in the melted butter. Barely cover with well-seasoned chicken broth. Cook slowly until liquid has all cooked away. Add seasoning. Continue cooking in the remaining fat until crisp and brown on the bottom. Turn and brown the other side. Cut in wedges. Makes 4 servings.

Sweet Potatoes & Yams

Sweet potatoes, which are natives of South and Central America, aren't potatoes at all—they're members of the morning glory family. Yams are a darker, sweeter, more moist variety of the sweet potato. One variety of sweet potato or another is available all year. They are very high in vitamins A and C.

SELECTING — Small to medium-sized sweet potatoes or yams are best. Look for firm, well-shaped ones with smooth skins. Avoid any with cracks or damp spots. Allow 1 medium-sized potato or 1/3 to 1/2 pound per serving.

STORING — Keep in a dry, cool area. Do not refrigerate. Will keep 2 weeks.

PREPARING AND COOKING — Sweet potatoes are excellent baked or boiled and used in numerous ways. To bake, scrub well and rub skins with a little oil. Place in a shallow pan and bake at 400°F 30 to 40 minutes. To boil, scrub well and cook unpeeled potato in kettle of boiling water, covered, until tender, about 20 minutes. Or if preferred, peel, quarter, and cook, covered, in a small amount of water until tender, 10 to 15 minutes.

SWEET POTATOES AND CHESTNUTS

4 lbs. sweet potatoes or yams
1/4 cup butter
1/2 cup cream, heated
1 can puree of chestnuts*
1 can plain whole chestnuts
parsley

146   Wash and peel potatoes. Cut into medium-sized pieces. Cook in boiling water until tender. Drain and return to heat to drive out any excess moisture. Put cooked potatoes through pureeing device while they are still hot. Beat in butter and cream. Put in top of double boiler over hot water until ready to serve. Break whole chestnuts into pieces. At serving time fold in chestnut puree and pieces. Pile onto heated serving dish and serve as hot as possible. Garnish with parsley, if desired. Makes 8 servings.

*Clement Faugier Puree of Chestnuts, flavored with vanilla, is available in super-markets in the gourmet foods section.

YAMS WITH RUM AND WALNUTS

1 lb. yams
3/4 tsp. salt
1/2 cup dark brown sugar
4 to 6 tbs. butter
1/2 cup broken walnuts
1 jigger rum

147

Select large red yams. Scrub and boil whole until tender. Cool and peel. Slice about 1/2 inch thick. Arrange one layer in a buttered baking dish. Sprinkle with a little salt, brown sugar and dot with plenty of butter. Add another layer of yam slices and continue as above until ingredients are used. Sprinkle walnuts on top. Pour rum over all. Bake in 350°F oven about 30 minutes or until hot and yams have a shiny glaze. Baste occasionally during baking. More heated rum may be added during baking, if desired. Makes 6 servings.

Spinach

Spinach originated in Persia and was taken to Europe by way of Spain. In England it was known as the Spanish vegetable. It, too, came to America with the colonists. Spinach is available all year around with the peak season being from March through June. It is rich in vitamins A and C, folic acid, one of the important B vitamins, and iron . . . just like Popeye says.

SELECTING — Look for bunches with crisp, dark leaves. Reject wilted, yellow leaves or untrimmed, gritty bunches. Usually sold and priced by the bunch.

STORING — Trim roots and wash in a sinkful of warm water. Lift leaves out, leaving the grit in the sink. Rinse in cold running water. Drain well and refrigerate in a plastic bag. Use within 3 to 5 days.

PREPARING AND COOKING — If pre-washed, it will need only to be well rinsed again just before cooking. Delicious and nutritious when cooked in a covered pan using only the water which clings to the leaves after rinsing.

SPINACH TARTA

12-1/2 tbs. butter
3 tbs. flour
1 cup milk
salt, white pepper, nutmeg
4-1/2 lbs. spinach
8 eggs
1/4 lb. bacon, diced
150 1/4 lb. grated Parmesan cheese

Melt 1-1/2 tablespoons butter in saucepan. Remove pan from heat and stir in flour. Season to taste. Pour milk in slowly. Return the pan to heat. Cook, stirring, until sauce boils. Set aside. Remove stems and thoroughly wash spinach. Cook in a deep pot using only the water which clings after washing. Drain well. Squeeze small handfuls at a time until dry. Chop finely with a sharp knife. Melt 3 tablespoons butter in a straight-sided saucepan about 8 inches across and 4 inches deep. Add spinach and mix well. Transfer buttered spinach to pan with sauce and mix well. Using the deep pan, make four 2-egg omelets using 2 table-spoons butter for each omelet. Turn the first 3 omelets out onto foil as they are made but leave the 4th one in the pan. Brown bacon pieces in a skillet. Add bacon and Parmesan to spinach mixture. Mix well and correct seasoning. Spoon 1/3 of the spinach mixture over omelet in pan. Cover with another omelet. Add another third of the spinach and cover with another omelet. Continue in this fashion until spinach and omelets are used. End with an omelet on top. Cover tightly with aluminum foil. Bake in 350°F oven about 30 minutes. Remove from oven and allow to stand a moment or two before unmolding. Cut into pie-shaped pieces to serve. Makes 6 to 8 servings.

SPINACH VARNAS

3 bunches spinach
3 tbs. butter
3 tbs. flour
salt and black pepper
1-1/2 tbs. sugar
2 cups half & half
3 eggs

Thoroughly wash spinach and trim away stems. Cook using only the water remaining on the leaves. Cool spinach. Squeeze small handfuls until very dry. Chop coarsely using a sharp knife. Melt the butter in a saucepan. Remove from heat and stir in flour. Season with salt and pepper and add sugar. Blend in half & half. Place sauce mixture in blender container. Add spinach. Cover and puree. Pour mixture into saucepan and cook over medium heat until it comes to a boil. Simmer slowly about 10 minutes. Boil eggs exactly 7 minutes. When ready to serve, place spinach in a bowl and garnish with halves of the boiled eggs. Makes 6 to 8 servings.

SPINACH CUSTARD

6-1/2 lbs. spinach
1/4 lb. butter
salt and black pepper

5 eggs
1/4 cup whipping cream
3 slices firm white bread

Thoroughly wash spinach and remove stems. Cook spinach over high heat using only the water which clings to it after washing. When thoroughly cooked, about 10 minutes, drain well. Squeeze small handfuls at a time until completely dry. Using a sharp knife, chop the spinach very finely. Do not grind. Melt 3 tablespoons butter and mix with spinach. Season to taste. Beat eggs and cream together. Mix well with buttered spinach. Transfer to a well-buttered souffle dish and set in another pan. Surround souffle dish with hot water. Bake in 425°F oven for at least 20 minutes, or until mixture is completely set, and a knife inserted into center comes out clean. Remove from hot water and allow to stand 5 minutes before unmolding onto a serving dish. Cut bread into cubes and fry in remaining butter. Surround spinach with bread cubes. Makes 6 servings.

SPINACH RING

5 bunches spinach	6 tbs. flour
4 eggs	1-1/2 cups milk
2 egg yolks	salt, pepper, nutmeg
4 tbs. butter	

Thoroughly wash spinach. Cook over high heat using only the water left clinging to the leaves. Drain. Taking small handfuls at a time, squeeze spinach dry. Beat eggs and yolks together in a large bowl. Place bowl of beaten eggs under meat grinder and grind spinach into the bowl. Mix eggs and spinach together well. Melt butter in saucepan. Remove from heat and stir in flour. Season to taste. Carefully blend in milk. Return pan to heat. Stir until sauce boils. Combine with spinach mixture. Pour mixture into a heavily greased 1-1/2 quart ring mold. Cover the ring with buttered waxed paper. Set the ring mold in another pan and surround with hot water. Bake in 350° oven about 30 minutes, or until knife inserted in center comes out clean. Remove ring from water. Allow to stand at room temperature 5 minutes before unmolding. Fill center with sauteed vegetables or creamed mixtures. Makes 6 to 8 servings.

SPINACH BARNET

2 lbs. fresh spinach <u>or</u>
    2 pkg. (10 oz. ea.) frozen leaf spinach
3 tbs. butter
2 large onions, finely chopped
1 tsp. Bovril

1/4 cup flour
1-1/4 cups strong beef stock
salt and pepper to taste
1 hard-cooked egg, sliced

If using fresh spinach, wash it several times to remove all grit. Cook just until tender using only the water which clings to the leaves. Drain and squeeze small amounts of cooked spinach tightly to extract every bit of water. (If using frozen spinach, cook according to package directions. Drain and squeeze dry.) Put dry spinach, through the finest blade of a meat grinder. Set aside. Melt butter in heavy skillet. Cook onions until nicely browned. Remove pan from heat. Add Bovril and flour. Blend well and add beef stock. Return pan to heat. Stir until mixture thickens and boils. Add ground spinach and blend well. Stir over low heat until thoroughly heated. Serve garnished with hard-cooked egg slices. Makes 6 servings.

Squash

Squash of all kinds has been growing in the Americas for over 5,000 years, and in all of that time they have changed very little. They are relatives of gourds and pumpkins. Summer varieties are a good source of vitamin C and the winter ones are high in vitamin A. All are low in calories.

SELECTING — Summer varieties such as crookneck, zucchini and patty pan, are best when small to medium in size. They should look fresh with shiny, smooth skin. Avoid wilted or bruised ones. Available all year with the peak season in June through August. Sold loose by the pound. One pound makes 4 servings.

Winter varieties such as acorn, banana and hubbard, should be heavy for their size with hard, shiny rinds. If cut, the flesh should look moist and of good color. One acorn squash makes 2 servings. Allow 1-1/2 pounds of the larger kinds for 4 servings.

STORING — Refrigerate summer squash in a plastic bag. Can be kept several days. Store cut pieces of winter squash wrapped in plastic and refrigerated.

Acorn squash keeps several days, unwrapped, in a cool, dry area.

PREPARING AND COOKING — Summer varieties do not require peeling. Scrub and leave whole, or slice as desired. Cook in as little liquid as possible, for as short a time as possible. Should be slightly crisp. Zucchini is good raw. Winter squash can be baked or steamed in large pieces, or cut up. Smaller ones such as acorn or Danish are usually cut in half and baked. Place pieces or halves in buttered baking pan, either cut-side up or down. If cut side is up, brush surface with melted butter and sprinkle with salt and pepper or other seasonings. Bake in 375°F oven 45 to 60 minutes. To steam, cook pieces in a steam basket over boiling water until tender, about 10 to 15 minutes. Mash and season as desired.

158

CHEESE-TOPPED SUMMER SQUASH

8 patty pan, crookneck **or** zucchini
1/2 cup boiling water
2 tbs. butter
1 tsp. seasoning salt
1/2 cup grated cheddar cheese

Cut squash in half. (Cut patty pan crosswise; crookneck or zucchini lengthwise.) Cook in boiling, salted water about 10 minutes or just until barely tender. Drain. Arrange in flat baking dish. With fork pierce centers of squash several times. Melt butter and add salt. Spoon over squash halves. Pierce again so seasoned butter will be absorbed. Bake in 350°F oven about 20 minutes. Top with cheese and bake 10 minutes longer, or until cheese is melted. Makes 6 servings.

STUFFED SUMMER SQUASH

Spinach Barnet, page 155
12 large patty pan squash
1 tbs. butter
2 tbs. grated Parmesan cheese

Prepare Spinach Barnet and set aside. Remove stems from squash. With a small spoon, hollow out squash centers leaving a fairly thick wall. Place squash in large skillet with butter. Cover and cook slowly until squash is tender. Turn once during cooking time. Remove and invert to drain thoroughly. Fill with Spinach Barnet. Place on a lightly greased baking sheet. Sprinkle with Parmesan. Bake in 425°F oven until heated through and cheese is crusty and browned. Makes 6 servings.

STUFFED ZUCCHINI

6 to 8 zucchini
1 tbs. butter
1 small onion, finely minced
2-1/2 tbs. flour
salt and cayenne pepper

1/2 cup milk
1 cup (4 oz.) grated Gruyere cheese
1 cup finely chopped ham
oil

Scrub zucchini. Cut them crosswise into 2-1/2 inch pieces. Remove pulp from centers with a small spoon, being careful not to go all the way through so there will be a bottom to hold the filling in. Rub the skins of the zucchini pieces with oil and set aside. Melt butter in saucepan. Gently saute onion until tender. Remove pan from heat. Add flour, salt and cayenne. Gradually stir in milk until smooth. Return to heat and cook, stirring, until mixture becomes very thick and boils. Add cheese and ham. Spoon mixture into hollowed-out zucchini chunks. Mound filling high on top. Bake in shallow pan in 375°F oven 15 to 20 minutes or until zucchini is tender and filling is nicely browned on top. Makes 6 to 8 servings.

ZUCCHINI A LA MENTONNAISE

6 zucchini
peanut oil
2 lbs. spinach
1 medium onion, finely chopped
4 tbs. butter
salt and pepper
2 cloves garlic
1 tbs. finely chopped parsley
1/2 cup grated Parmesan cheese
fine bread crumbs

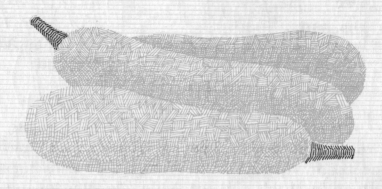

162

Cut zucchini in half lengthwise. Cut around each half 1/8 inch in from the edge. Make several cuts in the middle of the pulp, being careful not to cut through the bottom skin. Into a large skillet pour just enough peanut oil to cover the bottom of the pan. When hot add zucchini, flesh-side down. Cook gently about 15 minutes. Remove from pan and cool slightly. Then remove the pulp with the aid of a spoon, leaving the shell intact. Chop pulp. Wash spinach very carefully. Remove stems. Cook quickly in a large pot using only the water which clings to the leaves after washing. Drain and rinse quickly in cold water. Squeeze small handfuls at a time until completely dry. Chop coarsely with a knife. Melt 2 tablespoons butter in skillet. Add onion and cook slowly until soft. Season with salt and pepper. Add chopped zucchini pulp. Cook rapidly until all moisture has evaporated. In another pan melt remaining butter. When butter begins to brown, add spinach. Season with salt and pepper. Add garlic through a press, and chopped parsley. Cook 5 minutes. Add onion mixture and Parmesan. Correct seasonings and stuff zucchini shells. Place in buttered, shallow baking dish. Sprinkle with crumbs. Bake in 450°F oven 10 to 15 minutes or until nicely browned. Serve immediately. Makes 6 servings.

MARINATED ZUCCHINI WITH GAZPACHO DRESSING

8 (4 in. long) zucchini
1 small onion
1 clove garlic
3/4 cup olive oil
1/4 cup tarragon vinegar
salt and pepper to taste
pinch dry mustard, paprika
1 small tomato
1/2 green pepper, finely chopped
3 tbs. finely chopped onion
1 tbs. finely chopped capers
1 tsp. minced parsley
1 tsp. fresh basil (1/4 tsp. dried)
lettuce leaves for garnish

Scrub zucchini. Parboil in salted water about 8 minutes. Drain, dry and cut in half lengthwise. Carefully scoop out centers to remove seeds. Lay zucchini, cut side up, in large flat pan. Finely chop onion. Place in small bowl. Add garlic through a press and mix well with onion. Spread mixture over zucchini. Make a French dressing using the olive oil, vinegar, salt, pepper, mustard and paprika. Pour half over the onion-topped zucchini. Cover and let marinate in the refrigerator as long as possible. Chill the remaining French dressing. When ready to serve, remove zucchini from marinade. Scrape off and discard all of the onion-garlic mixture. Peel, seed and finely chop tomato. Combine with green pepper, onion, capers, parsley, basil, salt and pepper to taste. Stir in remaining French dressing. Arrange lettuce leaves on 8 individual salad plates. Place 2 zucchini halves on each plate. Spoon dressing over them and serve. Makes 8 servings.

ZUCCHINI PUFFS

3 slices provolone cheese*
2 cups shredded zucchini
3 tbs. chopped onion
1/2 cup bread crumbs
1/2 tsp. salt

1/4 tsp. pepper
2 tbs. chopped parsley
2 eggs
oil

Grate cheese in blender if available, or chop finely. Remove stem ends from zucchini and shred finely. Press out as much moisture from zucchini as possible with paper towels. Combine with onion, crumbs, salt, pepper, parsley and eggs. Put 1 teaspoon of oil in each of twelve muffin cups. Heat in 375°F oven 3 or 4 minutes. Carefully spoon batter into sizzling oil. Bake 20 minutes. Makes 12 puffs.

*Other cheese may be used, if desired.

166

BAKED ACORN SQUASH

3 medium acorn squash
1 tbs. oil
1-1/2 cups sour cream
6 tbs. dark brown sugar
6 tbs. peanut butter
garlic salt and black pepper
Tabasco

167

Cut squash in half lengthwise. Remove seeds. Rub surfaces with oil. Beat together sour cream, sugar and peanut butter. Season to taste. Fill squash cavities with mixture. Bake 1 hour in 350°F oven. Makes 6 servings.

ACORN SQUASH BAKED WITH RUM

2 acorn squash
1/2 cup hot water
4 tbs. melted butter
4 tbs. brown sugar
4 tsp. dark Jamaica rum

168   Wash squash and cut in half. Remove seeds. Place cut side down in a shallow baking pan. Add hot water. Bake in 350°F oven 45 minutes. Turn cut side up. Put 1 tablespoon butter, 1 tablespoon sugar and 1 teaspoon rum in each cavity. Bake 15 minutes longer. Baste once or twice. Makes 4 servings.

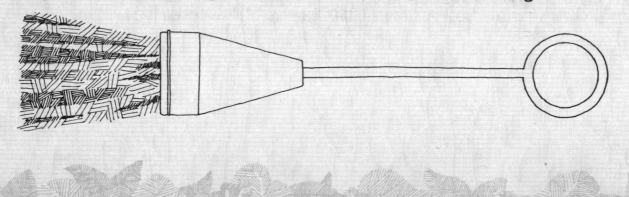

ACORN SQUASH WITH CREAMED ONIONS

3 small acorn squash
6 tbs. butter
salt, pepper, nutmeg
Creamed Onions, page 123

Wash squash and cut in half. Remove seeds and stringy portions. Place halves in shallow baking pan. Season with salt, pepper and a sprinkling of nutmeg. Place 1 tablespoon butter in each cavity. Cover with aluminum foil. Bake in 350°F oven 1 hour. Remove foil. Continue baking, uncovered, 1 hour longer, or until tender. Baste with the butter every 15 minutes. When ready to serve, fill each cavity with Creamed Onions. Makes 6 servings.

Unusual Vegetables

WILD RICE EPICUREAN

Wild rice isn't rice at all, it's a grass seed found growing wild in the northern United States. Difficult hand harvesting makes it extremely expensive.

1/3 cup oil
1/2 cup chopped parsley
1/2 cup minced green onion
1 cup sliced celery

1-1/2 cups wild rice
1 can (10 oz.) consomme
1-1/2 cups boiling water

1 tsp. salt
1/2 tsp. marjoram
1/2 cup sherry

Heat oil in a heavy skillet with tight fitting cover. Add parsley, green onion and celery. Cook slowly until vegetables are soft, but not brown. Wash rice well. Add to skillet along with consomme, water, salt and marjoram. Cover and cook over low heat about 45 minutes. Stir lightly with a fork every few minutes. If mixture becomes too dry before it is done, add a little more boiling water. When rice is tender and the liquid absorbed, stir in sherry. Leave uncovered and cook about 3 minutes longer, or until sherry has been absorbed. Makes 6 servings.

FENNEL A LA CREME

Also known as finocchio, fennel is related to celery which it resembles somewhat in appearance but not in flavor. Its flavor is sweet, mild and slightly licorice. It can be substituted for celery in much the same way celery root can be used instead of potatoes. The delicate flavor of fennel is especially delicious combined with this tasty sauce.

1 bunch fennel
4 tbs. butter
3 cups boiling water
salt, sugar, cayenne pepper
3 tbs. flour
bread crumbs
1/4 cup grated Parmesan cheese
1 cup reserved fennel stock

Remove tough outer stalks from fennel. Cut the remaining stalks into pieces. In a keep kettle melt 2 tablespoons butter. Add fennel and cook briskly

172

about 2 minutes, stirring constantly. Pour in water, salt and a pinch of sugar. Simmer 10 minutes, or until tender. Drain and reserve 1 cup of stock. Melt remaining butter. Remove from heat and stir in flour. Season to taste with salt and cayenne pepper. Add reserved stock and return to heat. Stir until sauce boils. Place in a flat, flameproof serving dish. Sprinkle lightly with bread crumbs and cheese. Run under the broiler until crisply browned. Makes 4 servings.

173

HEARTS OF PALM AU GRATIN

This unusual taste and texture sensation comes only in cans and only from Brazil, which seems to export as many hearts of palm as it does coffee beans. This delicacy is most often used in salads, but in Brazil it is sometimes used as garnish for cream of chicken soup, and from France comes this splendid combination. This is not a difficult recipe, but it does require several steps and will take time. We think it's worth the extra effort.

174

Mornay Sauce, page 10
3 cans (14 oz. ea.) hearts of palm
2 lbs. tomatoes
3/4 cup (6 oz.) butter
1 large onion, minced
salt, pepper, sugar

6 shallots, finely chopped
1 lb. mushrooms, finely chopped
1/2 cup white wine
2 egg yolks
1/4 cup grated Parmesan cheese

Prepare Mornay Sauce. Cover with plastic wrap pressed against the surface and keep warm. Empty hearts of palm and their juice into saucepan. Warm gent-

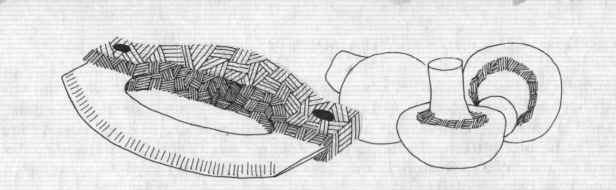

ly over low heat. Peel, seed and finely chop tomatoes. Melt 4 tablespoons butter in skillet. Add onion and cook slowly until soft, but not browned. Add tomatoes. Season with salt, pepper and a pinch of sugar. Continue cooking briskly until all juice has been cooked away. Set aside. Melt remaining butter in large skillet over medium heat. Add shallots, mushrooms and wine. When liquid has all cooked away, remove pan from heat. Quickly stir in egg yolks. Season to taste with salt and pepper. Remove hearts of palm from heat. Drain and cut in half lengthwise. On a flameproof serving dish make 2 beds, one of mushrooms and one of tomatoes. Lay hearts of palm on top and mask with Mornay Sauce. Sprinkle with Parmesan and place under heated broiler until browned. Makes 6 servings.

BRAISED BELGIAN ENDIVES WITH MORNAY SAUCE

Here is another salad item which is seldom seen cooked, but when the endives are young and sweet, their flavor is light and tempting. Extreme care must be taken in choosing endives, for unless they are pure white to pale yellow, they are apt to be old, bitter and offensive to most palates. Belgium endives, by the way, really are flown in from Belgium. This hearty dish goes especially well with rare roast beef or a broiled steak.

176

6 heads Belgian endives
5 tbs. butter
1/2 cup chicken broth
parchment paper
3 tbs. flour
salt and cayenne papper
1 cup (1/2 pt.) whipping cream
3/4 cup grated Parmesan cheese
dry mustard

Cut endives in half lengthwise. Butter a small, flameproof casserole, using 1 tablespoon butter. Lay endive halves in it. Add chicken broth. Place casserole over direct heat until the broth is boiling. Cover endives with buttered parchment, using 1 tablespoon butter to grease the paper. Bake in 350°F oven 20 minutes. Remove from oven. Drain and reserve the liquid. Add to it enough cream to measure 1-1/2 cups. In another saucepan melt remaining butter. Remove pan from heat and stir in flour. Season to taste with salt and cayenne. Add cream mixture gradually, blending well. Return sauce to heat and stir until it boils. Add 1/2 cup cheese and continue stirring until cheese is melted. Add a pinch of dry mustard. Correct seasoning and spread sauce over endives. Sprinkle with the remaining cheese. Bake in a 425°F oven until the sauce is bubbling and nicely browned. Makes 6 servings.

CREAMED KOHLRABI

Kohlrabi is widely cultivated and very popular in Germany, but in the United States it is one of the least known vegetables. Although it is a member of the cabbage family, it is a root vegetable with a texture somewhat similar to celery root. The small egg-sized bulbs are the most tender, but even those must be carefully peeled to avoid seeming stringy.

3 lbs. kohlrabi
2 cups beef stock
1 cup reserved cooking liquid
1 cup milk
6 tbs. butter
6 tbs. flour
salt and cayenne pepper
1/2 cup whipping cream
3 tbs. chopped parsley

Peel and slice kohlrabi knobs. Strip away the most tender leaves and mince them. Place leaves and slices in a small saucepan. Barely cover with beef stock. Cook 20 minutes, or until the slices are tender. Drain and reserve 1 cup cooking liquid. Mix with milk. Drain the kohlrabi thoroughly. In another saucepan melt butter. Remove from heat and stir in flour. Season to taste with salt and cayenne. Blend in liquid. Return to heat and stir until sauce boils. Blend in whipping cream. Add well-drained kohlrabi to the sauce and reheat. Serve sprinkled with chopped parsley. Makes 6 servings.

Index

*Nitty Gritty recipes

*Nitty Gritty recipes

                        *Nitty Gritty recipes

*Nitty Gritty recipes

Potatoes & Yams Finishing Touches The Paul Mayer Method Artichokes Celery Root Green Peppers Brussels Sprouts Cauliflower Asparagus Onions Cucumbers Eggplant Spinach Finishing Touches Carrots Cabbage Squash Leeks Artichokes Asparagus Mushrooms Eggplant Brussels Sprouts Cauliflower Cabbage Unusual Vegetables Celery Broccoli Green Beans Squash Mushrooms Onions Leeks Potatoes